Shining Mom... *wisdom of your soul – the divine "knowing" in your sp... core – that death is nothing to fear.*

— KATHY SANDLER
on behalf of The Elisabeth Kübler-Ross Foundation

In Shining Moments, *Georgia Weithe has written a powerful book demonstrating that we all have the power to choose what thoughts, what attitudes we put into our minds even in the face of death. It is a book filled with love and hope.*

— GERALD JAMPOLSKY, M.D.
Founder, The International Center for Attitudinal Healing and
Co-author, *A Mini Course For Life*

Shining Moments *is a valuable resource for everyone since we are all mortal. It shows us that in accepting our mortality, death can be the most significant teacher in our life.*

— BERNIE SIEGEL, M.D.
Author, *Prescriptions for Living* and *Love, Medicine and Miracles*

Shining Moments *is a life-giving essay about death, and that kind of paradox is laced through this very personal book. Writing about something that many of us regard as ugly, brutal, and terminal, Georgia Weithe reveals the beauty, the grace, and the new beginnings that death can bring.*

— PARKER J. PALMER
Author of *A Hidden Wholeness* and *Let Your Life Speak*

In Shining Moments: Finding Hope in Facing Death *Georgia Weithe speaks honestly, with amazing transparency, to herself, and allows us to listen in: it is a rare look inside a soul so like our own. I suspect that many people will, through her work, find that hope of which she speaks.*

— MARIANNE NOVAK HOUSTON,
Facilitator and Consultant, Center for Courage and Renewal

Shining Moments *is wonderful! It ranges from heartbreaking to philosophical; I enjoyed every bit of it, and felt it was extremely good to read at my particular time in life.*

— ALICE SPICER, AGE 90

In Shining Moments: Finding Hope in Facing Death, *Georgia Weithe supports our journey toward the profound truth that in accepting death we open ourselves to a deeper, richer experience of life. Using illustrations from her own life, and most profoundly insights from the time of her father's diagnosis and death from cancer, she provides lessons for those facing the death of a loved one. The book is a needed antidote for our death-defying culture.*

— CLAIRE HOLLAND, MSW
Former director Upland Hills Hospice, Dodgeville, Wisconsin

This has to be published! Shining Moments *could be a companion to anything Kübler-Ross has written.*

— NAN MILLER
Author, *Psalms for Praying* and *Journey to Love*

For individuals who need help navigating the river of grief, Shining Moments *provides guidance and support to keep them afloat. It is a resource every therapist should have on their shelf, to hand to clients in need.*

— SHIRLEY LIMBERG, MS, LCSW
Psychotherapist, Minoqua, Wisconsin

Shining Moments *is Georgia Weithe's moving and detailed account of how she accompanied her father through his dying and in so doing came to terms with her own mortality. Whether in training as a clinician or facing the death of a loved one, this book offers personal and helpful guidance from one person's journey.*

— PENNY WILLIAMSON, SC.D.
Associate Professor of Medicine,
The Johns Hopkins School of Medicine

Shining Moments *allows us to walk closely along with the author, through her fears surrounding death and dying. It offers Hospice caregivers valuable insight into this process of evolution from fear to hope, from the perspective of a family member. It reminds us to live fully, and to look at death with much more than fear, alone. It helps to create a place for dialog around the topic of death, and the attendant emotions and feelings that may come with the dying process... a worthy discussion in our culture and times.*

— CLAUDIA GEHLHAART, RN, CHTP
Former Hospice nurse

Shining Moments

Finding Hope in Facing Death

Georgia Lang Weithe

Reflections Press
Lone Rock, Wisconsin

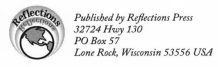

Published by Reflections Press
32724 Hwy 130
PO Box 57
Lone Rock, Wisconsin 53556 USA

Copyright ©2008 by Georgia Lang Weithe

Discounts are available on bulk quantities to corporations, professional associations, and other organizations. For additional information about the author and the book contact Reflections Press directly at toll free 888-604-5535, contact the author at shiningmomentsbook@gmail.com, or visit http://shiningmoments.net

The author gratefully acknowledges the permission to print
Elisabeth Kübler-Ross' quote granted by the
EKR Foundation,
www.elisabethkublerross.com and www.ekrfoundation.org

Publisher's Cataloging-In-Publication Data
(Prepared by The Donohue Group, Inc.)

Weithe, Georgia Lang.
 Shining moments : finding hope in facing death / Georgia Lang Weithe.
 p. ; cm.

 ISBN-13: 978-0-9790343-1-2
 ISBN-10: 0-9790343-1-0
 ISBN-13: 978-0-9790343-0-5 (invalid)

1. Death--Psychological aspects. 2. Spirituality. 3. Bereavement--Psychological aspects. 4. Weithe, Georgia Lang--Family. 5. Fathers--Death--Psychological aspects. I. Title.

BF789.D4 W45 2008
155.9/37
2007925504

LCCN:2007925504

Cover photo: istock   Author photograph: Scott Dietrich
Cover and interior book design: Peri Poloni-Gabriel
Knockout Design, www.knockoutbooks.com

Printed in the United States of America

Contents

Part 1

The Body Speaks and the Mind Remembers

Part 2

*The Body Speaks, the Mind Remembers,
and the Heart Understands*

Part 3

Finding the Path We're Already On

Dedication

For My Dad

When it was my father's time to die, he waited until I could fly across the country to be at his side. Since he had spent his entire life giving generously to family and friends, I'm convinced the timing was no accident. It was, rather, a profound act of love; his final gift to me. The last four days of his life, as he slipped into a coma, I stayed by his side and stared at his face constantly, searching for any sign that he needed help. I was holding his hand when he took his last breath, and felt I had assisted in his passage by handing him up to God. As a result of staring into the face of death, I underwent a powerful transformation. Gradually I have come to understand that although death took my father, it gave me a deeper and richer understanding of life.

From the moment I heard the news that Dad was dying, I wanted someone to lay out a map showing me the course of action I should follow. I called everyone who might possibly be able to tell me what to expect—how my father would behave, what he would need, and what I should do to help him. But nobody gave me the answers I was looking for. Instead, I was told again and again that each person is different and there was no way to anticipate the experience. Though I found this response frustrating at the time, now I know it was the truth. Nevertheless, if even one of those people had described in intimate detail their experience in facing death, it would have been tremendously helpful to me.

While navigating this unknown territory, I kept a journal to help me find my way. When I read through it after my father died, I realized it contained exactly the kind of information I had been seeking from others, but was unable to find. So I offer my story to help those who, like myself, have been terrified of death and who feel the need to have a conversation—even if it's only with themselves—about this phenomenon, which has generally become unspeakable. By sharing my experiences and the insights gained through them, perhaps I can provide you with a tool for courageously facing the death of others and the prospect of your own.

If you are accompanying a loved one on this journey, you cannot afford to be afraid. In the presence of the dying, we must not allow fear or rage to play itself out. There is a resonance that matches each emotion, and the frequency we maintain and project onto others must be chosen very carefully. We must exude the essence of faith and belief that will take the dying person to another vibration: inner peace.

For years Dad urged me to write a book, and I dismissed the suggestion by telling him I didn't think I could do that, because I had nothing to say, which was the truth. Now, for the first time, I feel compelled to write, and ironically it was his death that provided me with a context for my story.

I never expected that facing death would be one of the shining moments of my life. I have learned that death is a teacher and a friend, and I hope that what follows will be helpful to those seeking the light in the midst of what can seem a very dark experience.

Gratitudes

∽

I am so grateful for all the help I received along the way:

… to my Dad for giving me a story to tell, and to my Mom for her support of the project;

… to my husband Hartmut for his unconditional love and support, and our children Dawn and Andrew, who are my inspiration and my teachers;

… to Germaine Maiden, my dear friend, whose influence touched my soul and allowed me to become myself;

… to Kay Ortmans, for pointing *up* to remind me that we live in two worlds, and for her advice to "keep your head in the clouds and your feet on the ground";

… to Parker Palmer, for changing my direction by

pointing *down* toward the ground of my being, and helping me find the courage to explore my inner landscape;

… to Linda Boyd who was willing to talk to me about death when nobody else would;

… to Alice Spicer who gave me the hearty endorsement of an octagenarian, and the confidence to forge ahead;

… to Helene Barbara for the words "Shining Moments";

… to Jean Kitchen for her impeccable timing and superb editing;

… to Hospice and to Janet McShan, for the tender loving care she gave my father in the last days of his life;

… to the grace and the beauty of the land at Hilltop, which provided the peaceful environment that allowed me to listen and hear these words;

… and finally, I give thanks for the guidance and the guides who helped me along the way.

Georgia Lang Weithe
Bear Valley, Wisconsin
August, 2007

Introduction

∽

$\mathcal{I}$ have been preoccupied with death for as long as I can remember. All my life I have either been thinking about it in order to make sense of it, or trying *not* to think about it so I wouldn't *have* to make sense of it. What follows is the story of my own personal struggle to become comfortable with the idea of death and dying, but it's a story that involves every person ever born, because death is the final chapter in everyone's life story.

Death doesn't obliterate life; it is a unifying force that illuminates it and portrays it as real. Yet for most of us, it is the elephant in the room we are unable to acknowledge. Whether we're aware of it or not, death is the driving force behind most of what we do. On the one hand, we keep ourselves busy so we'll have something to show for our time on earth. On the other hand, we don't dare allow ourselves to become idle and risk being forced to think about why it is we keep ourselves busy. Everything we do is informed by the fact that our days are numbered. Death is the hidden agenda that we keep so well hidden, we are not even aware of it.

I don't believe that we are born with a fear of death. I know that my own earliest thoughts about it were not tinged with fear. The fear was acquired throughout my childhood in stages, from experiences I can recall quite vividly. I gradually became indoctrinated into the uneasiness of those around me, and the ultimate telling of lies, which pushed the story of the truth of my existence farther and farther away. For most of us, the end result of this process is that finally, lonely and without resources, we find ourselves struggling against the current of our lives, drowning in the misunderstandings.

I grew up in Chicago, where some of my first encounters with death involved finding dead birds in the street. Their lifeless forms evoked feelings of fascination and compassion, but not fear. Once, I kicked a dead pigeon six blocks to a plot of earth adjacent to our apartment building, so I could provide it with a proper burial. On another occasion, I performed last rites on my pet guppy. I awoke one morning to find it floating on one side, close to death. I put its bowl on the kitchen table, pulled up a chair, covered my head with a towel, and began to sing and recite prayers I had learned in Sunday school, hoping God would hear me and heal the fish.

God didn't hear my prayers (the fish died), but my mother did. I saw her peeking around the corner of the bedroom with the phone to her ear, chuckling as she described the solemn ritual that was taking place in the kitchen. I was too grief-stricken to be humiliated, but I was also not afraid of what was happening to my guppy.

The terror that eventually became linked to my perception of death began, I believe, with my parents' ardent attempts not to mention it. Dying is as natural as being born, although it's seldom talked about in our culture. In fact, the subject is to be avoided by every means possible. In spite of that, and even though I had never experienced the death of a family member or friend at an early age, I saw it everywhere I looked. I couldn't help thinking about it when the leaves turned brown and fell from the trees; when a spider drowned in the bathtub; when a baby bird fell out of its nest; when I watched the nightly news and saw bodies being pulled from collapsed buildings after earthquakes. These events are part of everyone's life, and when children observe them, strong feelings are stirred up that they need to talk about. Any feeling that can't be expressed becomes very powerful, and subconsciously I began to believe that if death could not be discussed, it must be too terrifying for words.

Then there were those times when the subject did come up, that I received the emotional equivalent of an electric shock, as signals were sent—some subtle and some not so subtle—that activated an alarm system within me. Those experiences created the wiring that sent out desperate and grave warnings as the topic of death was approached.

One such incident occurred when I was four years old. I was watching the rescue of a little girl, who was my same age, from a well into which she had fallen. She was alone at the bottom of a deep, dark hole, and I sat in suspense around the TV flanked by my parents and grandmother, waiting to see if she would survive. I felt my own family's tension as I witnessed the terror on her parents' faces while the rescue workers snatched her from the jaws of death. This made a huge impression on me. (I believe that part of the reason it was so frightening is because I was too young to have well-formed personal boundaries, and on some level I thought that I was the child in the well.)

In those days, television also periodically brought into our living room the tragedy of coal miners who were trapped when a tunnel collapsed. On more than one occasion when I was very small, the entire country was kept in suspense, waiting to see if missing miners would be pulled from the earth dead or alive. Sometimes the rescue operations we watched were successful and sometimes they were not. All of them paraded images of grief and expressions of pain and horror in front of my eyes, as their families reacted to their loved ones' terrible fate: death.

Another pivotal incident happened when my Aunt Ida and Uncle Joe came to dinner one night. They got into an argument and went into my parents' bedroom to continue their fight. Uncle Joe was diabetic and was eating everything he wasn't supposed to at the dinner table, and in frustration, Aunt Ida yelled at him, "I wish you were dead already!" Everyone gasped in horror, dropped what they were eating, and ran into the bedroom after them. Although I was a child and could not understand all the implications and nuances of this and the other situations, the message was coming through loud and clear: death was something very, very bad.

In fact, death is almost never portrayed as an accepted or peaceful experience. These snapshots of encounters with death, to which we're exposed when we're children, create a frightening imprint that remains frozen in our emotional field. Eventually nothing can convince us that it need not be feared.

The final "nail in the coffin," an event that imprisoned me in a state of fear and dread, occurred when I was about seven. It caused me to flip into anxiety so severe that for the next four decades, I would feel compelled to avoid the subject or else risk triggering debilitating panic attacks. My parents went to a funeral, and when they came home I asked them to tell me what death was like. Their reply was that death was like going to sleep. This is something parents should never tell their children. That night, I fell asleep and had a nightmare in which I dreamed I was dead and buried in a box under the ground.

Like most children, it never occurred to me (and it didn't occur to anyone to explain) that my body, when dead, would no longer be able to walk, talk, or breathe. In the dream, I was buried alive and I was suffocating. The terror I felt at being trapped in that coffin, with a lid on top and several feet of packed earth holding it down, still haunts me. When I pushed up I could feel the resistance of the entire world pushing back, and I panicked at the thought that there was no way out.

I bolted upright in bed and looked around, but the bedroom was pitch black. This, in my groggy state of mind, seemed to confirm that I was truly underground. There was not even the usual crack of light under the door from the bathroom night light across the hall to show me where I was. Nevertheless, the wisdom in my body prevailed, and I got up and ran out of the room. Much to my relief, I found myself in familiar surroundings, and the awareness of where I was and what had happened slowly penetrated my consciousness. That incident left me marked with an indelible fear of death, and I could not seriously face it again for many years.

When we are very young, we approach everything with an open mind, even death. Unfortunately, our early contacts with the reactions of those around us close us down and cause us to engage in avoidance and denial instead. Denial was the course I would take for many years to come—until my father was dying, and death wasted no time in teaching me what I needed to know. Then I found myself so completely enmeshed in the immediacy of its demands that I was compelled to live in the moment, to be strong and at the same time to surrender. Surrounded by death and its agenda, I was like a fly in a spider web: the more I tried to disentangle myself, the more tightly I was caught.

I had no choice but to succumb to the inevitable, since my overriding concern for my father's needs forced me to put aside my own fears. When I did, I discovered that underneath the fear, the rage, the pain and the conflicts, there is a current of energy that connects all the parts to the whole. When I climbed aboard the train and started this journey toward death, I began experiencing a truly remarkable and unexpected phenomenon. As my father was dying of cancer, amidst what felt like one of the darkest episodes of my life, there were moments when utter clarity descended upon me. In those moments, it was as if a light was shined on my soul, and the illumination revealed all the wisdom and understanding I needed to make sense of every situation. I call these moments and the insights they conveyed, *Shining Moments*.

The experience of standing still and looking death in the eye is incredibly powerful and demanding. In trying to describe what is essentially incomprehensible to the mind, there is no way to avoid entering territory that is beyond intellectual comprehension and using words that do more than merely engage the intellect. For that reason, I have spoken here with a voice I hope will bypass the ordinary tools of cognition and resonate with you through an "inner sense." In the pages that follow, you will hear that voice speaking its wisdom in the italicized passages.

*"It's only when we truly know and understand
that we have a limited time on earth—
that we have no way of knowing when our time is up,
we will then begin to live each day to the fullest,
as if it was the only one we had."*

— ELISABETH KÜBLER-ROSS

Part 1

The Body Speaks
and the
Mind Remembers

Chapter One

The Beginning of the Journey

*T*he winter before my dad became ill, I was waiting my turn in a doctor's office when I picked up something to read, just to help the time pass. I could not have imagined how that simple act of extending my hand and randomly selecting a magazine from the table could set in motion an inner awakening that would completely change the course of my life.

An article in *People* magazine caught my eye, and I became fascinated by the story. It was about conjoined twin girls, whose parents made the agonizing decision at birth not to separate them because one of them would have died. They had survived seven years of sharing a single torso that had two sets of shoulders and two heads. The more I read, the more appalled I became at the thought of two human beings going through life in this condition. I tried to imagine how difficult it must be for them and also for their parents, who were trying to raise them as "normally" as possible.

The girls were young enough that they could be protected from the outside world to some extent, but their parents undoubtedly had a painful appreciation of the complex problems facing these unique individuals. I read about how they were attending public school, were learning to read and write, were participating in sports, and were developing a social life. It seemed to me that they required an unthinkable amount of care and attention, both physically and emotionally.

My reaction to the thought of this type of existence intensified to the point of absolute horror. I wanted to spill out my feelings and exclaim to someone, "I read an article about conjoined twins who have one body and two heads!" But I couldn't, because I found their story so distressing that I wasn't even able to speak about them. So I never said a word to anyone, and the memory of those girls weighed on my heart like a stone. Every once in a while, when it was revived, I felt the pain of their suffering again, and I wished I had never seen the article.

Today, I am truly grateful. Even though we never met, as events unfolded, their existence had a very powerful influence on my own. It's miraculous how their lives provided a thread of connection throughout the circumstances of the next few months, which were some of the most important days of my life. I wasn't aware of it then, but years later I have developed the perspective to understand what was hidden from me at the time.

The following spring my father was diagnosed with terminal lung cancer and I found myself in a direct encounter with death for the first time. The conjoined twins receded into the background as my father's situation became the focus of my attention. While brushing his teeth one morning, Dad noticed blood in his saliva. This prompted him to make a visit to the dentist, who found what he thought to be a benign tumor at the back of his mouth. The dentist sent him to an oncologist, and it was the oncologist who dropped the bomb. Tests revealed that the tumor in his mouth was the metastasis of cancer in his lungs.

"Mr. Lang, you have cancer in your lungs and it has

spread to the liver. We could treat the lungs with radiation, and that might or might not help. But it won't change the fact that your liver is affected, and the therapy will cause some very uncomfortable side effects. I recommend that you have your children come and be with you and that you try to enjoy the time you have left."

Death's Intrusion into My Illusion

My first reaction was disbelief; then came anger. I briefly entertained the notion that my father had been unfairly singled out to endure this tragic fate, and it made me mad. I just could not grasp the reality that death comes to everyone at some point, and this was his time. In retrospect, I realize my reaction was not unlike the illusions to which many of us cling, because we're simply unable to accept death as part of life.

I thought I had made peace with death, but now that it could not be avoided, I realized I had not. As I grew up, I didn't consciously make efforts to ignore it. Rather, I found a way of framing life and death that felt true for me and provided a comfortable explanation. I embraced the belief that we are born because there are certain evolutionary tasks our souls must accomplish on earth, and opportunities to fulfill those tasks are continually put in our path. With this belief came a calm acceptance that, although bad things may happen to me, I could still find reason to rejoice and view those events as opportunities, rather than tragedies. My belief system could be summed up like this: "Everything that happens is for a higher purpose, we have free will that allows us to choose how we respond to events in our lives, and death is a beginning rather than an ending, because life never ends."

Running away from anything that threatens our survival becomes the pattern of our lives after birth, since self-preservation is the focus of all that we most immediately need to learn. But it is imperative that at some point we stop pretending we cannot see death's presence as a force in our own lives, or the integrity of our existence becomes compromised. It was becoming clear to me that I had raced for comfort after the panic-inducing experiences in childhood. Rather than wrestle with the discomfort created by the thought of death, over the years

I had replaced the emotions with ideas. I went right to the happy ending and skipped the story.

But in doing that, I had leaped over a great chasm filled with unexplored feelings. I was able to explain away death by claiming it was nothing to fear. However, *thinking* about death proved very different from truly confronting it, and when I was forced to do so, everything started to change. The intellectual comprehension was transformed into an emotional reaction, and fear of death began to overtake me!

Previously, I had thought that my life course was set. Meeting death on an emotional level, however, resulted in a total disruption and caused everything that had been neatly stacked to topple over. Where I once felt I was on solid ground, that ground was no longer beneath me. The beliefs on which I had constructed my philosophy of life were falling apart, and the foundation on which I stood was crumbling.

The situation was very troubling. Was I a hypocrite, living without integrity—or just naïve? I wrote in my journal,

"I must accept death, yet I am resisting and fearful. It feels like I am between lives; one foot is stuck in childhood with part of me facing backward, and the other foot is in the present ready to move forward. If I let go of the old patterns, I will cut the connection to the past and turn myself around. With feet planted firmly in the present, there is no place to go except forward, unless I want to remain permanently stuck. I am marching toward the end of my life, toward my death, and I must make peace with this fact. Although my beliefs about life and death seem to have chosen me when I was younger, now I have to breathe life into them by truly feeling this understanding. Part of me has to die in order to face this situation: the part of me that is afraid of death. It's hard to let go of the fear, but I must surrender to the knowledge that life on earth ends, because I'm watching my father slip away. If I truly believe that life goes on, then I have to face it without fear. If I don't, I can't live with integrity."

Sometimes, when fear overcame me, it felt like I was falling into an abyss with nothing to grab onto. In those moments, I realized that I was free to create any response to the situation that I wanted; the nothingness left all possibilities at my disposal. I dipped into my wellspring of resources and drew up courage to meet this unprecedented situation in my life, although I can't really say why. This experience taught me that every minute we are using our free will to make choices, and in so doing, creating the shape of our lives.

Death is an integral part of life, and I was beginning to understand that in denying the emotional repercussions of that basic fact, I was closing my eyes to a reality that was staring me in the face all the time. The implications of living in such denial were very deep, indeed. In choosing to make myself numb and blind to the truth, I was excluding part of my life experience, and consequently all areas of my life were affected. I was only partially alive! This realization prompted a great deal of soul-searching and reflection in which I examined my feelings and thoughts about death. In the process, I experienced a shift as it became clear to me that I *could* face death, and that I was willing to be guided by the experience.

I knew that my foot was no longer dragging behind, anchoring me in childhood. I had taken a step forward that had not only brought me into the present, but also completely changed my direction. Now I was turned around, facing the rest of my life. Now I was an adult in the second half of my life, heading toward my own death. This felt like where I was meant to be, and it was easier to let myself flow in the direction my life was actually going, rather than expend the energy required to resist and fight against its current. I knew that from then on I would be able to live with the peace that comes from embracing one's own philosophy of life.

At that point, I was able to accept death, although I still didn't know how to deal with it. Consequently, I spent many hours on the telephone reaching out to friends and acquaintances who had some experience with death and dying. I wanted each of them to tell me specific words to say and give me directions for how to act in my father's presence. I was frustrated when, with perfect unanimity, they all said that every situation is different because each person chooses to face death in his or her own way.

I didn't realize at the time that the questions I posed to my friends were naïve and unanswerable, and so their responses, which felt very unhelpful, frustrated me. In retrospect, I know they were right. It is true that each person dies their own unique death, which requires us to wait patiently for the terminally ill person to come to terms with their health condition and to conduct ourselves according to the rules they dictate.

As I was frantically attempting to gather information from those around me, one friend in particular was extremely helpful. She was the administrator of a nursing home who had shared the last days, hours, and minutes of life with many people. Linda created a metaphor putting death in a context that was a comfort to both my intellect and my emotions. She suggested our life's journey can be compared to a train ride, and that throughout our lives we delude ourselves into thinking we don't know where the train is going. When people are diagnosed with a terminal illness, they can neither pretend that they don't know where they are heading, nor that their stop is way down the line; it's getting closer too quickly for denial. But, while *they* have to acknowledge their destination, the rest of us perpetuate the illusion that we're going somewhere else . . . and some of us don't even acknowledge that we're on the train!

After searching for answers outside of myself for several weeks, I felt a stirring inside as the wisdom in my own soul awakened and started to speak to me. My *Shining Moments* had begun.

Climb aboard and ride; it does no good to pretend you're not on the train. Acknowledge that you are already on the same journey as your father. Look through the windows and begin to see what you're passing. If you know where you're heading, you won't need to make detours. Stay on course and don't allow yourself to be pulled off. Look carefully at what seems obvious and find the deeper clues you are seeking. Right outside the window are the answers to questions about life's deepest meaning. Don't be afraid to look. Buy a ticket and ride the train!

Dealing with the Diagnosis

We all struggled to comprehend what we were told. Dad was not a smoker! He had not been feeling sick! How could he be dying??? After exhausting every possible explanation, there remained only one: my father was eighty-four years old and his body had begun to shut down and start to die. His time had come.

Your father's time on earth has passed. He will begin to transform into a being of light. Lift him every step of the way with your heart's joy. Know that he returns to the Source of All Life, from where he came. This is the end of life, which you must contemplate. Do not turn away. See its miraculous powers and charms. It is a deeply moving experience. Ride with it and allow yourself to be carried along by every emotion. Wait patiently as the changes take place, and give him strength with your loving presence.

No one in the family was prepared for such a shock, and we found ourselves on an emotional roller coaster. In the beginning we grasped at any reason to be hopeful. We clung at first to the idea that a wrong diagnosis had been made, after that to the possibility that some treatment would help, and then we held out the hope that he would be able to live for a long time in spite of the fact that he had cancer. The ups and downs served a purpose; they were part of the adjustment we had to make to this new situation in which we found ourselves.

The first news was a terrible jolt that sent our feelings crashing into despair. Every time we found some reason to be hopeful, we pulled ourselves up again, but not quite as high as the time before; whenever each new hope was dashed, we didn't go quite as low as the last time. Eventually the ups and downs leveled off into a plateau from which we were able to operate without tearing ourselves apart emotionally. Finally there was nothing left but to accept the fact that he was going to die . . . and apparently rather quickly, as the type of cancer he had was considered to be very aggressive.

Your father waits to return from where he came. Be brave in the face of discouraging circumstances. Help comes in many ways and not always as you would expect it.

As you prepare for his death, you are shaping your own death experience. Those who know the art of letting go can prepare themselves with less difficulty for the task of letting go of earthly life. Be brave. You have experienced the ready availability of your courage. Use it. Be guided by your heart; you will be helped.

Open your soul to the loving presence of the One and allow death to share its teachings. The Great Equalizer spares no one. Time will dispel your fear; you will graduate to another level and capture the reality of your existence by knowing your father's experience. Shape your response to the situation out of the wisdom of your soul.

Journey Home

Within a week after my mother called and told me what the oncologist had said, I was on a plane heading toward California. Throughout the trip the words "My Dad is dying of cancer" played like a continuous tape looping through my brain. On the flight I felt like I was suffocating, and as a distraction, I made an attempt to strike up a conversation with the woman sitting next to me (secretly hoping she would have something reassuring to say). I asked her where she was from and why she was flying to the West Coast.

She replied that she was on a business trip, and when the conversation came around to me and I told her the nature of my trip, she did not create any openings for me to go into detail. She obviously found death an unsuitable topic for small talk, because she buried herself back in her magazine as quickly as she could, seeming relieved that she no longer had to interact with me.

It was going to be a long flight. I closed my eyes and found myself drifting back to the day I heard the news; I remembered experiencing the overwhelming feeling that *this should not be happening!* It had always seemed that a parent dying was something that occurred in other families, but not mine. I know I shared this attitude with many in my carefree generation. We grew up as part of the comfortable middle class, in families that had plenty of food and clothing, cozy and stylish shelter, and good medical care. Yes, being a baby boomer had definitely contributed to my feeling very unprepared for what I was going through.

The Context of My Life

It may be an oversimplification to say that a group of individuals who happen to have been born at the same time can be defined by lumping them together under a single label. However, those of us who belong to the baby boom generation emerged into a context that strongly influenced our lives.

We burst forth on the scene in an historical moment of collective exuberance, unleashed when World War II, with its long period of abstinence and deprivation, came to an end. While our lives are in many ways separated by disparate experiences, we have all been touched and affected by the introduction of television, the Cold War with its accompanying atomic bomb drills, the war in Vietnam, the civil rights movement, sit-ins, marches and protests, the assassinations of three heroic statesmen, the dawn of the space age, and the women's liberation movement.

Most of us born into middle-class families between 1946 and 1964 also experienced a factor that was critical to the development of our emotional and psychological landscape: growing up in a home with an intact two-parent family. There may have been many versions of that family, ranging from dysfunctional to life-sustaining and healthy. But regardless of its drawbacks and idiosyncrasies, the fact is that our parents were married, and we had homes we could come back to and families we could fall back on. Home was not always a place where we could count on being happy, but its mere existence provided a foundation on which to build a sense of identity and security.

In addition to the nuclear family, extended families played an important role in our childhood experience as well. Nearly every Sunday my mother, father, brother and I would get in the car and drive to my aunt and uncle's house for a weekly gathering. There we would bask in the warmth and familiarity of our family after spending the week largely in the cold company of strangers.

I found comfort in the weekly ritual, which included a seemingly endless ride out to the suburbs of Chicago, followed by the enthusiastic greeting my uncle showered on me as I stuck my face in the small pane of glass in the front door. Once inside, there was the good and abundant food we all brought and shared; the occasional spontaneous outbursts of dancing that erupted when Uncle Pat demonstrated the sound of his marvelous stereo to an appreciative (if slightly envious) audience; and the endless gossiping and storytelling in which the adults engaged.

In the midst of the clan, I felt protected and happy, and I was always reluctant to leave when evening rolled around and each small family circle drifted back together, said their goodbyes, and got into their respective cars to head for home. We did so, however, with the expectation and knowledge that the larger circle was there, waiting for us to take our place in it whenever time allowed us to make the journey again to Oak Park.

With a sizable extended family to step into, I knew where I belonged and I had a variety of perspectives from which to view and define myself. I was my brother's sister, my parents' daughter, my grandparents' darling; each of my ten aunts and uncles and eleven first cousins (with whom I played regularly) also provided me with information about myself and where I stood in relation to them. This gave me a wide patch of ground to stand on.

My place in that community of others afforded a base of experience from which I drew self-knowledge and the emotional tools needed to build relationships and create links to the world of which I was a part. Beginning in this small circle and stepping off its solid shore to wade into the unknown waters of life, my transition into the larger society was undoubtedly easier than for those growing up now, who frequently find themselves on the shifting sands of changing family structures. "I know where I stand" was a subconscious mantra threading its way through the fabric of my life.

When the sixties rolled around, the traditional family bonds began to unravel, but the shared experience of belonging to that unique American landscape created a continued sense of communal identity for baby boomers. There was an ebullient optimism in the air that had colored our view of life since early childhood, in part attributable to the feeling of elation that accompanied the end of the war and victory for our side. Our country's pride in having developed the atomic bomb fed a sense of superiority and invincibility, which increasingly pervaded the national consciousness. In school, we were told that the U.S.A. was the best place on earth to live, and that others envied our prosperity and freedom. While our cupboards were bursting with food, we collected dimes to send CARE packages to starving and less fortunate children in other parts of the world.

The economy grew and was driven by government money in the form of the G.I. Bill, which provided inexpensive mortgages, paid college tuition, and made loans to start businesses. With inflation low and earnings high, many couples realized the American Dream of owning their own homes, and most of those homes had a TV in the living room and a car in the garage. Just as oxygen was part of the air we breathed, we were inhaling with every breath an extraordinary sense of self-righteousness, and that created an atmosphere of patriotic euphoria. In our belief system, virtue was measured in terms of the abundance of material objects; God was on our side and we had the goods to prove it!

One of the by-products of those good times was a tendency on the part of our parents to be overprotective. All parents try to shelter their children, but ours were especially concerned about shielding their offspring, because the Great Depression, two world wars, the Holocaust, and the threat of nuclear war had a profound effect on them. They tried to keep us from knowing the tragedy, death, and destruction that had shadowed, and in many cases, directly touched their lives. Out of that shadow we emerged into the light and grew in the radiance of peace and prosperity. We had food, shelter, clothing, health care and entertainment. We benefited from breakthroughs in medical science that enabled us to combat diseases that had plagued our ancestors, allowing us to live longer and healthier lives. If our parents wanted to protect us and provide us with a better life, as most parents do, then they were definitely in the right place at the right time.

I belonged to a privileged group of people who, for the most part, were insulated from nasty things like death and disease. I had seen people on TV whose lives were disrupted by such events, but it seemed impossible that this was happening to me.

Offended by Death

As Americans, we are raised to believe that we're a privileged few chosen to live in the best country on earth. For that reason, there seems to be no room for doubt or imperfection, and the disfigurement that comes with age is an especially offensive affront to our sanitized lives. We've turned our backs on messy events like death and aging by worshipping beauty and youth, and we've erected barriers to hide the evidence of the passage of time. We're not willing to abandon the idea that we can improve on nature, so as waves of destruction wreak havoc with our bodies, we mount a defense.

We play harder, wear increasingly youthful clothing, dye our hair, and surgically erase the signs of wear and tear that time has wrought on our bodies. This need to transmute the original creation of life forms may stem from the shared belief that there is nothing we can't do when we put our ingenuity and know-how to work. We can stop the march of time if we want to . . . we're Americans!

Message to Baby Boomers: It's Time to Mend the Quilt

All these experiences have become woven together, creating the patchwork quilt that makes up the emotional fabric of our lives. But lately, as we have gotten older, signs of wear are becoming apparent. The seams are coming apart and the strong threads that once held the pieces together are starting to unravel. We saw it slowly beginning to deteriorate but we just stopped looking . . . postponed the mending job for another time. However, looking away doesn't change the fact that the holes are getting large and obvious. It's time to mend the quilt!

We live in a culture that denies the inevitability of death, and denies it more vigorously than ever before. We have developed the misguided belief that if we simply eat the right foods, take the proper vitamins, wear the correct athletic shoes, and follow an excellent exercise regimen, we will manage to "conquer the enemy" and somehow avoid death. The notion is widely held that those who do succumb, have lost "the battle," due to a flaw in their strategy or technique. This attitude carries unfortunate consequences for both the individual and our culture at large.

An unwillingness to face death prevents us from living our lives completely, never experiencing the full range of possibilities that life holds, because we're only willing to acknowledge one end of the spectrum. Then, when death does manage to invade our lives, we become pariahs and are forced into isolation. I wanted to talk to everyone about what was happening to my father when he became ill, to discuss how I felt and receive some guidance. But very few people would give me permission to bring up the subject, because most of us are simply scared to death of dying.

The time has come to recognize our position in life and to take a stand where we belong. In the swirl of materialism, we have been sold a bill of goods. We have willingly consumed a sales pitch proclaiming that life has no more purpose than to be extended as long as possible, and that we can give our life meaning by relentlessly pursuing pleasure in the time we have on earth. It's no wonder that dismay greets us when we look in the mirror one day and realize there is not much left of what we deemed so important.

For our parents, there was no looking back. They pointed us towards the future, and on the wings of prosperity and abundance we have been chasing toward it from the moment we could stand. Propelled by our parents' love and drive to provide the security that their world never had, we grew up in a protective bubble, and we've been more shielded from death than any other generation. But now we're running out of future. Death is getting closer, and soon there will be nothing left to do but accept it.

Chapter Two

Face to Face

The wheels bumped along the runway and jolted me back into the present. My fellow passenger's discomfort had heightened my own, and I was trembling when I got off the plane in Orange County, California, on a bright May afternoon. Was it possible this was a movie about somebody else's life? This was where people landed who were going to Disneyland! Couldn't I just get on a bus and head toward Fantasyland, instead of Leisure World where my parents lived?

Be thankful for your trip. Elevate your emotions to gratitude for the opportunity to see your father again and pay tribute to his contribution to your life. His goodness flows in your veins and is a source of support and direction in your life. Tap into the Source of All Goodness and give thanks for his influence. Waste no time on sadness. This is a time to rejoice. His difficult earthly journey is coming to an end.

You can help your father by maintaining your spiritual connection to him throughout your visit. Do not become overly emotional and subject him to more than he can handle. Peace will reign over him as he passes through his transition, and your gentle, reassuring presence will communicate what he needs to know.

Your lack of fear in this situation is what he needs. You can find relief from fear by taking refuge in the peace that comes with death, rather than fearing it. Fill your body with love—draw it down and dwell in your spirit at those times when fear would overtake you. In this way you can change your own vibration and feel the power of prayer.

> *Remind him that life is a mystery, filled with miracles that should never be forgotten. Birth and death are the most outstanding, and make the greatest impression, but underneath every interaction is a thread of connection to a greater Source of Understanding than what appears on the surface. Don't focus on isolated scenes; direct your gaze on the connections between the lines so you can find the bigger picture.*

I left the terminal (another reminder) and searched for the shuttle that would drive me south toward San Diego. The two people who shared the van with me were at the other end of the emotional spectrum. They were lovers just arrived from England, who were totally absorbed in one other and very excited about their impending tour. We were delivering them to a rental agency where a recreational vehicle awaited them; they were going to spend the next two weeks driving and camping along the California coast. How I envied them and longed to share their light-hearted joy.

As we traveled toward their stop, the driver asked me why I had come to California. I told him that my Dad had terminal cancer and I didn't know how long he would live, so I was coming to spend an undetermined amount of time with him. My words landed like a heavy weight on the high energy being emitted by the couple in the back seat. They stopped cooing and chattering and expressed their sympathy. The driver's gentle response set me at ease, as he congratulated me for coming to my parents' assistance in their time of need. He said he thought it was sad that many children, under the same circumstances, abandoned their parents, and he felt I was to be commended. I appreciated his kind words, and was especially grateful for his lack of discomfort and willingness to discuss the subject.

We arrived at Leisure World and I showed my gratitude by giving him a very large tip. With trepidation I headed down the sidewalk, toward my parents' home. Should I mention Dad's illness right away? Would I start to cry the minute our eyes met? I wanted to be strong to provide him with support, and not be in need of it myself. I rang the bell and my mom opened the door.

Dad was sitting in the living room fully dressed, not looking at all like a person close to death. He greeted me cheerfully and inquired about my family. He listened eagerly and intently to every detail as I filled him in on all of our activities. Occasionally I attempted to bring the topic around to how he was doing, though I didn't directly ask about his fears or how he was coping with the situation. He shrugged my questions off and never revealed his innermost thoughts. When not engaged in conversation, he would sit staring into space, privately contemplating his fate.

Wait patiently for your father to come to terms with his health condition. Begin to care for his spiritual needs by elevating his awareness of the transitory nature of earthly life along with your own growing awareness. Prepare him for his journey through your understanding and your love. He will become more sensitive to the peace you send him as his transformation becomes more complete. Connect with his higher spiritual sense, for that will overtake his physical body as he passes on to the next phase. Prepare him with your love, and his increased consciousness of what awaits him will become a source of comfort and peace.

You will become more grounded with every passing day in this reality; your father's earthly life is over and he continues on the other side. His passage will go quickly and he will be grateful for the lack of pain. In his mind he is adjusting to the possibility that his end is near. Have no fear—he will be helped and guided when the time comes. Plain words, gentle talk and loving embraces; these will be his needs in future days to come. Remember your mother and pray for her strength in facing the loss that lies ahead of her.

I spent the days doing what I could to be helpful. I took my mother shopping, did the laundry and helped with the cooking. In the evenings, when everyone had gone to bed, I inevitably found myself contemplating death. I was floating in another reality, marking time while waiting for death to reveal its hand.

Continue to search for the wisdom of your soul in this situation; it has all the answers you are seeking. Surrender your fears and hand them up to God for safekeeping; you do not need them. Do not be sad for him or you will drag him down into earthly emotions, which are not helpful. Grant your father the hope of great joy and relief awaiting him on the other side.

Ascend ever higher rather than sinking into despair. Catch the wisdom and comfort that are available. When you feel yourself slipping, draw on the wisdom of your soul, to which you have ready access, and peace will be with you. Spiral upward into heavenly domains—not downward into earthly emotions that will drag your father down and inhibit his ascent. Assure him his work is over and has been successful. All come to earth for a time to accomplish a purpose. His task has been to spread love, and he has worked great miracles. Many have been transformed through his loving example.

In the stillness of those nights, I repeatedly came face to face with myself, and the truth of my existence. Once, while lying in the dark and feeling acutely aware that my father's time on earth was slipping away, I found myself contemplating our relationship to time.

Race Against Time

We cannot know or accept death without understanding the true nature of life: there exist mysteries for which there are no solutions, and there are ways of viewing life that create solutions where there are none. Each one of us is a willing partner in perpetuating the illusion that all life is subject to our definition of time. Immersed as we are in a constant contest with the clock, we have become slaves to the notion that our lives are a series of beginnings and endings, and that between each, we're running a race.

We have overlaid a grid of patterns on our life experience, creating an artificial construct based on the hands of a clock. Twelve numbers with two hands moving across them hold the power to rule our lives. We fashion contests with time in which we delineate tasks to be accomplished, and we set deadlines by which our goals must be achieved. When we succeed, we convince ourselves that we have been victorious and have managed to conquer time. Each little victory increases our sense of power and adds to the belief that if enough energy is spent on a task, anything is possible—including staving off death. The perpetual push to beat the clock creates an aggressive quality that dominates our behavior and locks us into a pattern of pushing away or of reaching rather than receiving. Consequently, many of the natural lessons our life experience can bring to us are lost, for only in a state of receptivity can understanding, wisdom, and meaning find us and enrich our lives.

Seeing our lives dissected into modules interrupts our vision of the entire picture; we lose sight of where we are, where we've been, and where we're going, until the larger plan of our natural lives becomes obscured. The true rhythm and pattern, its ages and stages, become engulfed by the illusions we construct. In times past, when we lived together in groups of diverse ages, when entertainment consisted of social gatherings filled with conversation, when we measured our position in the community by responsibilities that were defined by the family group, we had a better grasp of the passage of time and of the fact that with age, our lives ripen and change.

But regrettably, we have become focused only on beginnings and endings, and nothing that happens in the middle seems to matter. There is no sense of becoming—only arriving. There's no sense of being alive as we walk through each experience. Just a breathless feeling that there isn't enough time to get everything done, so we must take every shortcut possible to arrive at the finish line. Never mind how we got there.

Time to Surrender

It was in these nightly periods of contemplation and meditation that I was able to collect and compose myself so I could face the next day. We had gotten to the stage when we were no longer dealing with doctors, opinions, decisions, and effects of treatments: only death was left. Nothing I had experienced before had prepared me for the sudden, inescapable reality that death was coming to claim my father and that he would have to surrender, because there was no way out.

As all of us move through life, the feeling that we're going somewhere propels us forward, although we're not necessarily aware of what we are heading toward. Babies are creeping toward childhood, young children are moving toward adolescence, teenagers are rushing toward adulthood. Adults are striding toward success and the trappings that define it—power, money and material possessions. We're all on the same train, speeding toward our goals, while passing by a multitude of possibilities regarding how to achieve them. Following his diagnosis, I felt the momentum of my dad's life stop suddenly and abruptly, as if a wall had been thrown up in his path.

A devastating aspect of being told someone has a terminal illness is the sudden and irreversible feeling that the many choices life offers are shrunk dramatically. In my dad's case, after giving up on life-prolonging treatments (judging the disadvantages and discomfort as outweighing any advantages), we were faced with only the option of how to fill each of the days that were left. At first that felt like no option at all; it seemed the life choices were so reduced as to be nonexistent, or at best, pathetic.

But in fact, the scope of possibilities that both dying

people and those around them can choose from are wide-ranging and varied. I learned that in every moment, for each of us involved in the experience, a choice remained. We could either embrace death and allow it to take us on its journey, or we could resist and refuse to face the experience, remaining insulated by our own fears.

My father chose neither to fight what was happening to him nor to acknowledge it. He knew his cancer was incurable, but each sign that his health was deteriorating—loss of appetite, loss of weight, loss of energy—did not signify the end to him. He acted as if each new stage of the illness could continue indefinitely or was potentially reversible, and that he might start feeling better eventually. He was walking the fine line between clinging to hope and denying what was happening to him.

I found that very little of my previous life experience was relevant to what I was up against when facing death. I could have avoided, feared, fled, pretended—but standing in the presence of death commanded me to reject any illusions or any tricks my mind wanted to play on me. I chose to look it in the eye and face it, because defense mechanisms seemed so useless, and even fear could offer no way out. Fears are phantoms that haunt us and throw shadows on areas of truth. But this was a truth that I could not hide from and could not shake: Dad had arrived at that destination for which we're all headed—the end of our lives.

All my life I had been aware of death, but I never dwelled on it for very long because there was no need to. I acknowledged its presence and then brushed it aside, glancing only occasionally at it out of my peripheral vision. Now it was right in front of me, staring me in the face, and it felt as if there was nothing to do but stare right back. The strength I gained from making this effort changed my life.

Death Can Move Mountains

You are blessed by the presence of the great teacher— death. It transforms the lives and the soul power of the individuals who are facing it if they are willing to look it squarely in the eye. Do not pretend that you cannot see its presence as a force in your own life, or the integrity of your existence will be compromised. This is a core issue: the real understanding that death will come to you, too. You need not be frozen by the prospect, but can allow yourself to expand into the awareness of the next phase of life. Rejoice, for you have found the key to living with the knowledge of your own death.

There is nothing in our lives that has the capacity to remove fear, replace old habit patterns, generate new thoughts, and release creativity like the experience of looking death in the eye. Crammed into a moment's willingness to accept the phenomenon of death and decay is a power of renewal and rejuvenation that is unimaginable. All the force of our efforts to resist the existence of death is unleashed in a torrent of creative energy when the roadblocks we erect in our own path are removed.

Gather all the strength it takes to face death, and know that great comfort rewards this endeavor. Massive amounts of creative energy become dammed up in the attempt to stop the course of nature's flow. When the dam suddenly breaks, we can hope to ride the current of rushing water, trying not to lose our balance as we hang on for dear life. Or, we can start opening the floodgates ourselves so the force of the water doesn't come as a surprise and knock us over. When we drop the effort to deny the existence of death, living becomes easy.

True choice abounds here. We can know that death exists if we choose to, and our ability to live with integrity is equal to our willingness to face it. When we play hardball with life, we risk crashing into walls of denial and suffering black-and-blue bruises of the spirit if our attention slips and we look briefly away. We cannot pull a veil over our eyes and still expect to have clarity of vision. Looking through a clouded lens distorts the definition of everything we attempt to see; removing the filter reveals the truth and beauty of all aspects of life. Remaining always vigilant against having the awareness of death slip into our consciousness will sap our strength and zest for living. The sweet surprise of our lives is waiting for us behind the door we have slammed shut.

> *Be prepared to meet death at all times. It is always nearby and its presence illuminates your life experiences. It is a teacher and a friend. Refrain from fear. If you reach for it, you will make contact. There is no need to introduce negativity into your thoughts regarding death. Do not ground yourself in earthly cares or concern yourself with what you cannot change. This is the larger plan for all human life—to descend to the earth plane for a period of existence and return to the Source.*

A Cherished Moment

My brother was scheduled to arrive the week after I did, and in the time I had alone with my dad, I was determined to have a long-overdue conversation. I desperately wanted to tell him how much he had given me throughout my life and how grateful I was.

There was one other thing in particular I wanted to share with him; something I wrote not long after arriving, which was inspired by a child I didn't even know. My parents had shown me the photograph of a friend's young grandchild, and I was touched so deeply by it that I couldn't get it out of my mind. I kept seeing the light radiating out from the baby's eyes, and it occurred to me that I could offer my father some comforting thoughts about death by drawing his attention to the other end of life.

Ideas poured out of me and I wrote them down on a beautiful card, then waited for the right time and place to share it with him. I felt this conversation should happen in uplifting, peaceful surroundings, so I continually tried to orchestrate a trip to the ocean. He always appreciated the beauty in nature, although he spent very little time outdoors, but every time I suggested we take a drive, something prevented it. I believe that at this point in his life, the thought of deviating from his routine frightened him, and we were never able to go. Nevertheless, the compulsion to have this talk grew very strong in me, so one night I abandoned the idea of going to a special place and asked Mom to give me a few minutes alone with Dad.

> *Restrain yourself no more; allow the love and emotion you feel for your father to pour forth and surround his being. He will feel your support and be comforted by it. Plunge into the depths of your heart and uncover the vast eternity and boundless loving character of the great Unknown Creator; there you will find your father.*

We went into the bedroom together and I shut the door. As I began to share with him what was in my heart, I could feel he was worried that I was going to force him to confront emotions he was not prepared to deal with. I let his uneasiness go right past me and began to tell him that I wanted him to know he was one of the greatest teachers I'd had in my life. He sensed where this was going and adjusted to the intensity since it was heading in a direction that didn't feel unsafe.

I told him he was my most important teacher, because he had shown me who I am. He taught me that love is at the core of my being, and he did that by loving me. When I told him, his eyes grew wide with surprise; he gasped and said, "I had no idea!" How sad that he didn't know. How sad that I had never been able to communicate this to him; but ours was a family that was too inhibited to discuss anything related to our true feelings. I realized the time for restraint was over, and if I didn't seize this opportunity to pour forth all the love I felt for him, to say all the things that had gone unsaid over the years, I would never have the chance again.

In the twenty minutes we spent in that room, I believe his heart filled to overflowing and he understood that I would be eternally grateful for his gift of love. I gave him the card, and left it with him to reread if he cared to do so. In the course of that visit, I saw him pick it up several times and read these words:

Dear Dad:

I want to share with you some thoughts I've had about the miracle of life. First we're born, we live our life, and then we die. Birth is a miracle we rejoice in, so it doesn't make us afraid. But it's a great mystery—just like death. Can you imagine that your life began as a seed planted in your mother's womb, and that you grew inside her body for nine months, then passed through the birth canal out into this world? The journey you were on is as mysterious as the journey of death. Yet, as you were guided into the unknown, you knew no fear because you were able to trust. Can you imagine that happened to you? Can you imagine you never existed before you made that passage? You came from God and return back to the Source at the other end of this journey we call earthly life. Have the faith and trust of the little child who you once were; let go of all fear, and trust that you'll be guided back from where you came.

Look into the eyes of a child and you will see where it has been—and where we are all meant, in the end, to go.

These thoughts have been a source of comfort to me, and I hope they are also to you.

Your loving daughter,
Georgia

When we emerged together from that room, there was a light in his eyes that I don't remember seeing before. I'm sure it had been present and visible at times in his life, but I could not recall it. It was the light of self-realization; the love at the core of his being had been stirred by my loving gesture and was radiating out, reflected in his eyes.

Beaming, he walked straight to my surprised mother, embraced her warmly, and gave her a kiss. I hadn't seen him do that for years. His love was overflowing and his impulse was to share it with her. She was greatly relieved to see his joy, because she didn't know what the outcome of our private meeting was going to be. I cherish the memory of that look in his eyes, and of the entire event.

You have created a path for your father to follow. Your words have erased doubts and fears and given him the courage to move on to the next phase. Remain joyous, loving, and light in your attitude toward him. Continue to lift his spirit as long as he remains on the earthly side of life. He has known the beauty of your love and will be comforted by it.

Return

> *Leave behind you a trail of wonder and awe for the experience of death. It is not necessary to be dragged into the depths of those around you. Connect more strongly with this higher knowing and identify yourself as you really are: human now, but more than human, as all on earth are. Deliver your father from fear by reminding him that he has a body, but he is much more than a body. He is also a loving spirit that will live on.*

After remaining with my parents for two weeks, I decided it was time to return to my own family. Dad's health was deteriorating but it didn't appear that death was imminent. He was eating very little, losing weight, and had no energy, but those were all expected consequences of the cancer. He never mentioned the words death or dying, and it was clear no one else was supposed to either. It was all very new, and he needed time, it seemed, to get used to the idea. My mother was also in denial.

Realize this is happening to both of them. Be careful what you say to your mother so you don't upset her. She is afraid of the truth, but this is a truth she cannot escape. Be gentle and loving and kind. Listen carefully to both of them so you can meet them where they're at. They require continued loving responses. Treasure these moments with your father, as you will not see him like this again. Continue to lift him and hand him up to the Source. He is in loving hands and his spirit will be kindled by the Brightness as his body continues to fade. Bring him to the understanding that you are available to come back at any time. When his time draws near, invite him to call you so you can be present with him at the moment of his passing.

Mom didn't want to talk about what was happening, so I was surprised when she agreed to allow me to take her to the funeral home, where we made all the necessary decisions and arrangements in case Dad should die while I was away. I further anticipated her needs by discussing business matters with their insurance agent, consulting with the hospice caregivers, and meeting with Dad's doctors.

Bring to your father's awareness again today your appreciation of the love he has given you. Cancel all negative thoughts that may arise. Be patient and loving and give him comfort with your presence—palliative care for the dying. Tomorrow upon parting tell your father you love him. You came with hope for a future life; leave him with a reminder that life continues. As you take this next step, remember not to be afraid. Your inner guidance will carry you along.

While tending to these practical matters, I cared for my father by being present with all my love for him, and by being a compassionate listener and supporter. Plain words, gentle talk, and loving embraces were what I was able to offer him during those two weeks, and I left feeling that I had done the best I could.

Pray for your father daily and he will feel your strength. Channel love into his body and give thanks every day for the lack of pain. It is a wonder. Awaken your love for the spirit in his body and strengthen your awareness of its greatness. See him not as a fading human but as a growing spirit that will find peace and rest as time continues to pass. Place your love and trust in the working of God's miracles. Your father is fading away but his spirit emerges triumphant. Let him go, and release him back to God from where he came. Play your cards lovingly and allow more freedom and joy to envelop you as you contemplate his transition.

Continue to release him and give thanks for the help he is receiving. It is not your task to be his guide, or to be present and take control of his journey to the other side. Release him and know it is meant to be. You have done all you can. Continue to be loving and pray for him. This is the support he needs from you now. Return to your life and your marriage and bring your new passion for living to everything you do.

The night before going home I wrote,

"I will always be grateful for the love you have given me."

Chapter Three

Waiting

*B*ack home in Wisconsin, I asked what I should do now, and the answer that came was "wait."

> *Wait for him to summon you. Plan to be at his side when he dies. You will know when the time has come. Lift his heart and soul heavenward and help him leave behind the fears of the living. Carry him upward on the wings of love. Lift your spirit and soar with him to the heights that are familiar to your soul. Build confidence and love into his departure and you will repay the confidence and love he has instilled in you, which will carry you throughout your life's journey on earth.*

While waiting, I tried to resume my normal existence. I planted the garden, cooked for the family, and read everything I could on death and dying. I felt I had so much to learn, but soon discovered I didn't have to go looking for the lessons; they found me. I became preoccupied with the question of how it came to be that when we were children, we perceived death as nothing to fear, yet by adulthood we had become mortally afraid of it. The answer seemed bound up in the development of our personalities, so I proceeded to examine the evolution of our fears by picking them up like a tentacle and tracing them back to their source.

Our Relationship to the Body: the Container that Holds Our Fears

Although we are not born with a fear of death, we are predisposed to it. At any given time we are both living and dying, so fear of life ending becomes our inheritance when we enter the world. At birth, our primary task is to learn to inhabit our bodies and define ourselves in terms of their boundaries. Meanwhile those same bodies are simultaneously tracking an irreversible course toward the moment of their death, at which time we will become disembodied and those boundaries will dissolve. This underlying paradox of our existence requires that we accept the inevitable, yet not abandon our responsibilities in life; that we learn to steer our course, while allowing the course we are meant to take to steer us.

When we begin our life's journey, the orientation of our being is toward where we have come *from*, not where we're *headed*. Babies are glowing with a light that is reflecting what they have just seen. Their eyes show us where they have been, and where we are all, ultimately, meant to go. In time, they learn to shift their focus and train their attention to life on earth.

We come into the world with a mind that is uncluttered by words. A baby knows nothing of the community into which it is born—the language by which those around it communicate or the rules by which they live. It can't wait, however, to make sense of its surroundings, because the mind is by nature very curious and outgoing. By comforting and supporting the tender new being and allowing it to reach out, parents convey to their child that the world is a safe place, and that moving about and exploring brings rewards of wonderful and awesome proportions.

If children are pushed too hard to achieve milestones of growth and development, they push back, creating a resistance and rigidity that are contrary to the flexibility and receptivity needed for learning. However, with gentle care and nourishment of the soul's basic needs, the wisdom of the body develops and speaks to the individual's drive to gather and collect new information, which will ultimately allow the creativity within to flourish. Our lust for knowledge propels us toward a flowering of understanding which, when met with no opposition, persists in unfolding throughout a lifetime.

But the same culture that fosters the development of its young children also creates deep confusion in them, when early in their lives it begins sending messages that cause a disconnect between their bodies and their minds. The roots of all knowing begin with the body—it's the eye of the needle through which all facets of knowledge are drawn. By encouraging children (girls especially) to flaunt their sensuality long before allowing them to be sexual, we force them to at once acknowledge and deny the existence of their bodies, which can be profoundly perplexing.

In order to live our lives with integrity, we must begin with the ability to be comfortable and accepting of who we are. If we dissociate ourselves from our bodies, we begin our life's journey with a lie that multiplies and distorts our perceptions. As we continue adding layer upon layer to that already shaky foundation, we create identities that are fragile and potentially warped. An existence built upon a lie cannot lead one down the path of truth.

Our understanding of who we are and our place in life stems from our ability to inhabit our bodies and experience them as the point from which to commence integrating the vast amount of information that streams toward us from the complex environment into which we're born. As infants, our mouths and tongues receive nourishment, and our souls are nurtured by touch. The seed that is planted in the physical form grows and evolves limb by limb, until finally we develop the capacity to connect all the sense impressions we've been taking into the body with the ideas that have floated past and through the mind.

The very first associations between our selfhood and the larger community have to do with the body and pertain to definitions of right and wrong. When we're taught to control our elimination according to social conventions, from that point on we cannot maintain our original identity and wholeness, because we're no longer free to surrender to our natural impulses. Society makes a claim on our minds and spirits when it takes control of our bodies; a net has been thrown over our free will and we have been caught.

In the process of learning how to play the game by society's rules, we become interwoven in the social fabric, and soon we're an integral part of the whole. As we mature, we embark on a quest to find our own individual shapes; this involves a pulling out and away from the fabric, but we always remain connected by a thread.

Gaining conscious control over our impulsive behavior is a continuing task throughout our lives. As we grow, we cannot give in to our desires to sleep, to eat, to move or to play; each urge becomes constrained by the social environment in which we are raised. Every time we conquer another natural impulse we strengthen our identification with the body and become ever more distanced from our true nature and original spirit. We are taught that the energy with which we exercise self-control is our inner strength. Eventually the effort of overcoming our natural tendencies becomes the framework on which we build our social identity.

The body becomes the container in which we learn to guard our spirit and our vulnerability, but as we increasingly identify with the container, we lose sight of the contents. The more effort required to maintain the integrity of the shell, the more we associate our existence with our physical form, and the more that *beingness* and *nothingness* become the two poles between which we deposit our terror. The container and its maintenance become the focus of our existence, so we cannot contemplate its destruction. We find ourselves making desperate attempts to prevent any signs of deterioration, because if the container begins to crumble, where will we be?

We are taught that we can delay its inevitable decay, and to that end, spend a staggering amount of money on products that cater to our desire to stay young, or at least to look that way. We embrace the pursuit of a youthful appearance to the point where our wrong attitudes enslave us. In a frantic attempt to stave off the aging process, we pluck, remove, transplant, tighten, paint, dye, inject, jog, press, lift, train, tone and resort to countless other time-consuming procedures that shackle us to rituals designed to support the intense denial that we have constructed in our minds.

But in fact, chasing after youth will never reclaim the seconds that have gone by. We cannot move forward if we have chained ourselves to the past, and each plastic surgery performed shackles us to moments that have already been lived. Turning back the clock is impossible; we will always be living in the present, and pursuit of where we have been rather than where we are heading inevitably becomes a source of pain.

As long as we are preoccupied with the container, we will continue to feel empty. When we allow the true meaning of our lives to flow through us and let ourselves be taken on the ride of our lives—only then will we know the highs and the lows, the fears and the joys, the beauties and the truths we are meant to contain. And like it or not, one of the truths we are meant to contain is the fact that we are going to die. We are not meant to live forever, and whether or not we believe that life goes on after death is immaterial to the fact that physical death is pursuing us from the moment we are born.

As we are taught to focus on surviving in the world, the whole underlying pattern of our life's journey from birth to death recedes into the background and becomes invisible. However, if we look with detachment at the evolution of the container that holds our being, we see a process no different in its elements and progression from the development and growth of a flowering plant. In infancy we are a tight bud, a bundle of possibilities, a spirit that is unique and waiting to express itself. If carefully cultivated, our ideal form takes shape as we unfold slowly through childhood and start to grow.

Eventually, the swelling and opening into the fullness of a blossom occurs in early adulthood, when the peak of our physical beauty is in bloom. There's a gradual fading of the bloom as youth declines, while we continue to develop and branch out in many different directions until our life has run its course. Finally, we begin to shut down our systems and shed the form, followed by decay and return to the soil.

The Body Speaks
and the Mind Remembers:
the Body Knows How to Die

We don't dare delve into the truth of our existence, which the body knows but the mind is too terrified to contemplate. Instead, we transport ourselves out of our bodies and construct a deception for our reality, until the time comes when the firewall of illusion we have created is shattered by the truth that can't be denied: life on earth ends.

When death comes upon us it joins the experience of the body with the mind's ability to name it, to make sense out of it, to attach meaning to it. If we have spent our entire lives hiding from what we have always known, the awareness will come crashing in on us with all the force of the effort we have expended in order to hide from it.

The body is continually speaking to us throughout our lives, and we can use our free will to acknowledge or ignore its statements. Too much time is spent frantically trying to harness the mind and drive it in the opposite direction from the truth. We try to forget that we are getting older and losing our shape, that our parts are wearing out, and that we are heading for ultimate physical destruction. But beyond a certain point we can no longer fool ourselves, and the longer we resist, the more the pain increases. The body knows how to be born, how to evolve into the different stages of life, and ultimately it will know how to die.

We are terrified of dying because it is the one time in our lives when the body will have its say, and we are forced to listen. Like a ghost or fearsome monster, the presence of death shakes us into the awareness of decay and destruction. This, in spite of the fact that we have throughout our lives cultivated a denial of the truth and forced this awareness into the deep recesses of territory that is too terrifying to enter.

We tread lightly around reminders of death's existence. But the body speaks and the mind remembers: the body knows how to die.

Fear of Feeling

A downside of our comfortable and easy lives is that we've come to scorn life's complexities and even deny their existence. Throughout the time I was growing up, the prevailing atmosphere in the country was unparalleled optimism. Taking cues from the Hollywood movies I watched every week, I learned to link my inner life to happy endings and tried hard to avoid emotional pain. I attached my feelings only to peak experiences by refusing to dwell in the valleys, and the consequence was a fear of the dark side of life. I have not gone down this path alone. Many Americans seem obsessed with happy endings and are so afraid of *feeling* that they, too, skim along the surface of their experiences.

But by turning our backs on every experience that is not charged with entertainment and bliss, we pay dearly. There's a bland quality to an existence that seeks nothing but pleasure. If we insist on embracing only one side of life, we exclude ourselves from the richness and variety of the human condition. Only by taking risks can we reach the highest possibilities life has to offer; the price we pay for excessive caution is the diminishment of our spirit's sense of wonder and the feeling of being truly alive. Ultimately, we cannot make sense of a world where we register only the highs and do not acknowledge the lows.

Without feeling the full range of human emotions, our journey through life makes contact with only a fraction of its real possibilities.

We want everything to be easy, fast, and fun—but we're caught in a dilemma. As we strive for increasing pleasure, we don't dare experience its full intensity lest we open ourselves up to the trap of feeling its opposite: intense pain. We can never relax as long as we must be on our guard, maintaining a constant watch to prevent our true feelings from sneaking in and overtaking us. Under the influence of drugs, we numb ourselves to all but the narrowest spectrum of feeling. We eliminate everything that could be experienced as uncomfortable or would require some effort to overcome. With no highs and lows, the accents in the symphony of life have been reduced to nothing more than whimpers, and we experience only the middle range.

Then, when death knocks on the door, there is nowhere to hide, no possibility of switching to another channel. The sudden trauma of having to confront the deepest waves of feeling attached to our existence evokes great pain and fear, and we cannot shift from being emotionally neutral to being propelled into the stratosphere of feeling without a deep sense of shock. We are thrown out of our familiar orbit with terrifying force. The intensity of emotion that surrounds the dying experience causes our lives to become grounded in the myth that associations with death must be avoided at all cost.

Chapter Four

The Call Comes

$\mathcal{O}$n the third of July, my mother phoned to say things were getting very bad. When I received the call, I lost my equilibrium and scrawled in my journal,

"Please help me. I'm so afraid. How will I be able to be with him. Oh God! Where is my faith? Is everything I believe in fake? Where is my integrity in this situation? Dear God, please help me!"

Your integrity is at the core of your being and will flow outward from the center if you do the dance of life. Bend gracefully and follow God's lead in the dance. You will know what to say and do. Your compassionate and loving self will take over and provide the strength and comfort you need in the situation. In the end you must hand yourself up to God; this is practice for your spirit's own letting go. Fear of death can only hold you if you allow it to do so, so give it up and be saved from the pain. You can choose your response in this situation. The light at the end of the tunnel is waiting for you. Rush through it to the other side.

The next day, the fourth of July, we were in the middle of a celebration, eating burgers and apple pie at a neighbor's house, when my son came speeding down the road on his bicycle to say that Dad's hospice nurse had called. I had asked her to notify me if she thought death was near, so I could be with him when he died. I made arrangements to leave for California the next day, and again I was consumed by fear. I had never been around a dying person. Would I be terrified? Could I handle it? What would I say to him? Immediately the guidance started to flow:

You will find the words you need. You have shed a layer of fear and now you will find that your strength will be there. Capture this moment of peace in your heart and allow it to grow. Gain strength from seeing the bigger picture. Be reminded that everything you have needed has always been given. Let this be your source of comfort today.

Forgive yourself your weaknesses. Behave as a daughter who is losing one of the pillars of strength in her life. You cannot reclaim him. You cannot save him from physical death. It is his time. Hold him in reverence and love and respect. Your holding will calm him and give him courage. Be in awe of his beautiful being; do not stray from this image.

Be gentle, loving and accepting; hold him to allow his soul to reach for its rest and comfort. Do not try to teach him any lessons. Invoke the power of his own Self through a path of non-interference. This is not a time to activate the mind. Reach his soul through the energy channels on which he will be transported. Sending the energy and love to him, you go before him and prepare the way.

You must work through the fear of death and become familiar with the peace associated with the experience. Peace will come to your father and his rest will give you comfort. Do not imagine that his passage is uncomfortable for him. The transition is easier than you think. In his deepest knowing, he is aware of what you have tried to convey. Lift your spirits and be comforted. He is not alone, and your prayers are assisting.

I felt very fragile as I packed my suitcase and prepared for my departure the next day. I was weighed down by my own anguish, and also by the thought that Dad was undoubtedly suffering, knowing what was happening to him. In this fragile condition I began my journey. As I sat in the airport while waiting to board the plane, more help and guidance streamed through.

Be not swept along by emotions that can serve no purpose but to drag you down into the depths of despair. You have so much to be grateful for. Death is a great teacher. Give thanks for the love that surrounds both your parents and the protection from pain that your father is already receiving. Rejoice in his dying to earthly life—it is quiet, gentle, and inevitable. He passes through the portals into the care of loving guides who will show him the way. You have done your part to lift him up and care for him. He is blessed; draw strength from this awareness and don't lose faith.

Elevate your emotions and allow gladness and gratitude to God to fill your heart

. . . for this time,
. . . for his guides,

> . . . *for the lack of pain,*
> . . . *for the love he has given,*
> . . . *for God's help and mercy.*

Panic!

With a small gesture, my seatmate on the airplane showed himself to be a very kind man—for which I was extremely grateful. He reached over the boundary of reserve and into territory where indifferent strangers don't normally venture when he helped me remove my sweater so I could settle into my seat more comfortably. This unexpected act of kindness opened my heart and dissolved my inhibitions so that I wanted to turn to him immediately and tell him my dad was dying. I hoped that if I poured forth my confusion, uncertainty, sadness, and grief, he would reach out to me with compassion and help me settle comfortably into that situation, as well. Reminding myself that people don't want to hear about death, I checked this impulse and said nothing about the nature of my trip.

To pass the time I began writing in my journal and found comfort in the words of wisdom that came to me:

You are guided in the direction of peace. Hope is all around you; strengthen your awareness of it at this time. Your father awaits your arrival before he passes over. You will come in good time. Know that he is being held; he needs only to let go of his physical being. Encourage him with your loving acceptance of his condition. Words will not be needed. Your resistance becomes his—your lack of resistance becomes his as well. Hold him in love and you will bring him peace.

This is your gift to the person who has brought you the peace to which you retreat in your life; the knowledge that love is at your core. Touch him with everlasting love and again awaken in him this awareness. This is not done through words, but through your loving presence, thoughts and prayers. You will see the power of prayer work miracles. Have faith; you will be given what you need.

> *He is aware of your coming and is comforted by the thought. Bless him with the growing inner calm and strength that you feel. Your heart will reach out when you see him and deep compassion and love will fill your being. You will never be the same for the experience.*

An hour into the flight, something so startling captured my attention that I could hardly believe my eyes. In the bulkhead seats across the aisle, a mere five rows in front of where I was sitting, I saw the curious sight of two unusually close and oddly positioned heads. They were bobbing over the seat back in an awkward position, which looked vaguely familiar. Suddenly, the memory of a picture I had seen returned to me, and I knew I was looking at the very girls I had seen in the magazine three months earlier. *THE CONJOINED TWINS WERE ON THE PLANE!*

I panicked! In my vulnerable condition, I couldn't stand to see a fly that was injured because I suffered its pain, and here I was locked in this small space with those girls who had been an unspeakable source of torment and distress since I read about them. This could not be happening!

I could not escape, though I desperately wanted to do so, and I didn't know how I would survive this experience. It was horrifying that to add to the agony I was already in, I had to share this small compartment with those two human beings, seemingly bound in inexplicable suffering, who had haunted me for months. They didn't look like they were suffering, though; they were actually bubbling over with excitement because they were on their way to Disneyland. I was in too much misery, however, to perceive anything but the complex and painful aspects of their situation.

I writhed in discomfort when they walked down the aisle to the restroom on their one pair of legs, and turned to the gentle man sitting next to me to point them out. In his tranquil frame of mind, he was awed rather than shocked by their situation. He marvelled at their existence and thought the experience of being so close to another human being must be truly remarkable. He also expressed amazement at the ability of the human spirit to rise above the most adverse circumstances and carry on. But I could appreciate none of that.

Being preoccupied with death as I was, I found myself wondering how they would die. Could one die before the other? What would that feel like to the remaining twin? Would it be a comfort to die with someone else? I was only able to see the dark side of their lives, and I suffered greatly as a result of their presence. At that time, I had no idea how positively I was actually being touched by them, or that being reminded of their existence was a gift that I would benefit from for the rest of my life.

Family Ties

When we landed, I called Lou and Libby, my dad's first cousin and his wife, who had offered to drive me to my parents' home. While waiting to be picked up, I watched other passengers bound joyfully off planes into the arms of friends and loved ones who whisked them away to beaches, amusement parks, movie studios, and surfside cafes.

There was no sign of the conjoined twins, and I forgot about them for the time being while my thoughts turned again toward my father. Driving to Leisure World, the conversation was awkward, as I felt unable to make small talk. I thanked the cousins for being available to my parents, and to me. With a conviction that reflected the strong values of their generation, they quieted me by saying, "Don't thank us. We're family. That's what we're here for."

Many times in the weeks to come I would rediscover what it meant to be surrounded by family—an experience forgotten by many of my generation who had grown up in a nucleus of relations, but had eventually cut ourselves adrift and started a different life amidst fresh circumstances and people. At this turning point in my life, as relatives began to gather and reminisce, I felt a huge sense of loss because I had withdrawn from the family circle.

Mom and Dad and their siblings and cousins grew up together in a neighborhood in Chicago, where their parents had formed a community with other immigrants who spoke the same language and practiced the same customs. Listening to their stories, I realized that these people not only shared the present, but they had a history as well; and because the roots of their connection went all the way back to childhood, they were very deep and very strong.

Uncle Norman laughed as he told how, when he courted his wife, Molly, my dad would stick his head out of the window every night at ten o'clock and demand that his baby sister come upstairs. She was seven years younger and Dad kept a close, protective eye on her. There were many stories I had never heard before: about enlisting and serving in the Army together, about life during World War II, about cars they owned that had to be cranked in order to start them, about neighborhood baseball and card games.

Aunt Faye told of the extra bedroom that my grandparents made available to whichever one of their six children had most recently married. I heard how Mom and Dad had to vacate the room, which they did reluctantly, when Molly married Norman.

As I listened to them recount the tales of their common past, I wondered what stories I would have to tell my own children. Certainly none would have the poignancy and depth of these people who had shared life and death over a period of more than fifty years, and who continued to be there for one another, giving and forgiving, until the ends of their lives. I realized how, by "liberating" myself of the often cumbersome weight of family ties, I had denied myself the richness of those connections.

The Final Days

I got out of the car and walked slowly toward the moment I had been dreading, saying a silent prayer as I approached the house . . . "Please prepare him to pass over to the other side. May the beauty of all that awaits him seep into my father's awareness, and let the fears of the living play no part in his transition." The door was unlocked so I walked into the living room. Throughout the trip I had been bracing myself for the first seconds of this encounter with Dad, since we both knew why I had come. The questions racing through my mind were the same ones that tormented me three months before: "What will I say to him? Will the first moment our eyes meet be so poignant that I won't be able to hold back my tears?"

Once again I was surprised to see him fully dressed and not looking like a man close to death. He was sitting on the bed watching his beloved Chicago Cubs play baseball when I walked in. Our eyes met, but I took my cues from him and neither of us acknowledged why I was there. In the presence of death's power, it seemed futile for me to rebel or quake with fear. I wanted to remain calm and accepting of what was happening, because I couldn't bear the thought of adding the pain of seeing his daughter break down to whatever other burdens he was carrying just then.

His mind was still clear and sharp and he remembered details of my previous visit three weeks earlier. He wanted to know how everything was going and asked pertinent questions about what my husband and the children were doing in my absence. I told him about my brother spending the weekend with us, about the garden, the cats, and the birds at our bird feeder. I was a bit confused because I thought he would be in a much greater state of decline than this. I didn't know then how rapidly his condition would deteriorate in the next few days.

After our chat, the first thing I did was arrange for the

rental of a hospital bed, which was delivered in a matter of hours. I could see that my dad's body was becoming very inflexible and he could not find a comfortable position lying down, especially when he coughed, which was happening more frequently. When the hospital bed arrived, he settled in and was able to raise and lower himself with the electronic controls as needed.

The hospice staff had been urging Mom to rent a bed, but she hadn't done it. She was somewhat paralyzed by the situation and needed me there as much as he did.

At six o'clock that evening, a nurse's aide sent by hospice arrived to help with his care. Patricia bathed him and fed him a bowl of soup. He fell asleep very early that evening and woke again around midnight. He woke up repeatedly and could not get comfortable, so we called hospice and asked what to do. They recommended we give him some of the sleeping pills that had been prescribed.

In the morning he told us they had made him sleep, but that they had caused him to be anxious and to hallucinate all night long. He was exhausted and miserable. I felt terrible that he had been subjected to this unnecessary pain and we called again to find out what we should do in the coming night. Janet, his nurse, came to check on him and suggested that we give him only Tylenol, since that seemed to help him sleep and he had no allergic reaction to it. He was extremely relieved to have been given the okay not to take the unpleasant drugs.

I stood at the foot of his bed and watched the interaction between Dad and Janet. Although his speech was slurred and difficult, he joked and kibitzed and was very glad to see her. She was warm and gentle, and lovingly caressed his face with her hand. When it was time for her to leave, she noticed there was a tear in the corner of his eye, and she asked if his eyes were bothering him. He told her they were not bothering him; he was crying because he had to say good-bye to her.

In the midst of a chaotic period, when everything he knew began to fall away, Janet appeared as a tender, understanding, and consistently loving presence to him. He seemed to know he would not see her again, and in fact, that was the last time he was conscious when she came to visit, and it was the only time I saw him shed a tear in those final days of his life. I will never forget the deeply moving connection I witnessed between my dad and his wonderful nurse.

Hospice workers are often the only companions dying people have who are capable of riding through the storms of their illness with them, willing to calmly face each new turning point without fear. Janet was exceptionally loving and gentle. I had a little chat with her before she left that day, and in the course of our conversation she said, "I believe in guardian angels. I'm sure your father, Sidney, will be one of mine."

All that day I sat at his side and held his hand as he drifted in and out of consciousness. While watching him sleep, I was reminded of what it was like to hold his hand when I was little. Dad was a towering six foot five inches, and he had to stoop to reach me. I felt like I was stretching up to touch a giant when I raised my arm in order to make contact. With my hand completely surrounded by his, I never felt more protected; the love and security his touch engendered allowed my soul to reach into uncharted territory and experiment with new ways of being and expressions of Self. As a child, he handed me the security I needed to live up to my potential and try on my identity.

At four o'clock in the afternoon he surprised everyone

when he suddenly became very alert. I took the opportunity to tell him what had just been going through my mind. I said that when I was small and reached up to put my tiny hand in his, I always felt very safe. He had not spoken the entire day, but that remark launched a talking spell. He said, "Speaking of size . . ." and began telling how tall his father and brothers were, and what size shoe each of them wore. He said that he had the biggest feet of all of them, size 14, a fact that made him laugh.

After that humorous introduction, he struck a more serious note. He told me who the three most important people in his life were. The first was a person who had launched his career as a salesman. He had spotted Dad when he was a very young man working in a clothing store on Maxwell Street in Chicago and asked him if he wanted to sell electrical appliances. That was the beginning of a long and distinguished association with Hyland Electrical Supply Company. (Dad noted with pride that he had a plaque on the wall commemorating twenty-nine years of service to the company.) His second most important influence was a man in the army who had arranged for him not to get shipped overseas during World War II.

Mom was the third.

After twenty minutes of recalling major events and people, he fell quiet. It was clearly a recounting of some of the high points of his life, and an acceptance of the fact that it was coming to an end, although he never said that. In the middle of his stream of words I was desperately wishing I had a tape recorder handy, but if I had tried to locate one, I would have missed some of those precious moments. It's a scene recorded indelibly in my heart.

Death Comes

He fell back to sleep after that and never completely regained consciousness again. The last verbal communication we had took place later that night and was one of the most poignant moments of my life. From time to time, as I sat by his side, I said, "I love you, Dad." I wasn't sure he could hear me and it didn't matter. But he let me know he heard me one last time when, without opening his eyes or even moving his lips, he managed to mumble the barely distinguishable words, "I love you, too."

> *Your father is homeward bound. You can help him on his journey by handing him up to God. Offer your prayers and include a remembrance of his soul. Surround him with hope and anticipation of his future life. What awaits him is peace and fulfillment and rest. You cannot bring him back so do not try. Release him. Place your trust that all is well in the hands of the Creator. Every cell in your body knows this truth. Do not rewrite the script with your own agenda. Remember to hand up your fear and trust that all is as it must be.*

I prayed, "Please hold this dear soul in your hands and carry him to his place of rest."

The next morning, Tuesday, Janet returned to take his vital signs. She said they were very weak and predicted he wouldn't last the afternoon. Wednesday was her day off and she very much wanted to be on duty to be with him when the end came, so she was glad that he was going to slip away on her watch. Things turned out differently, however. Two very important people in my father's life were due to arrive the next day; his son and his sister. I kept telling him that they were coming, even though he was unconscious, and his heart continued to beat. Janet said he could not possibly hang on for another day with a blood pressure reading of 80/60.

Accept the coming event and know that peace and rest await him on the other side. Pray for his soul to be carried away in peace; those who love him and who have gone before are guiding him. His heart beats weakly in his breast and his conscious mind floats between the two realities. Lift him up—increase your attention on the upward direction. Blow new life into his hopes for an afterlife and eternal rest.

He was still alive when my brother arrived Wednesday afternoon. Three hours after that, against all odds, his heart was still beating when his beloved sister, Molly, flew in from Chicago to say goodbye to the last of her four brothers. I'm confident that he waited until they had arrived. They spent some time alone with him and eventually went back to their motels for the night. I was determined to stay at his side until the end. I had the feeling that he needed someone with him, and I could not abandon him in his time of need.

Play the role of the loving guide and bear witness to the teachings of death. There is no reason to be afraid. Let go of your fear and witness the miracle of transformation. Life goes on. Life continues. You cannot stop the change. Your heart speaks and you know. Your thoughts only serve to confuse in this situation. Abandon your thoughts, lift up your heart, and pray for your father's survival after death.

For the first two days as I kept vigil, I held his hand. On this day, I sensed that in some way my life energy was feeding him, and that if he was going to make the transition, I needed to let go. So I did that, but stayed right at his side, telling him I loved him and sending him encouragement and support with mental rather than physical energy.

Do not weigh yourself down with fear. Clear away the weeds and allow the beauty of your soul to express itself. Be still. Quiet your thoughts and allow the experience in. Sail on it like a ship. Let it carry you like a wave. Know the comfort of its gentle rocking motion. There is no pain here but that of your own making. Your father is riding the wave of death, which will carry him into new life. His sails are set—his course is known. Blow wind into his sails and help him along.

With all the family gone, I lay down in my parents' bed, which was next to the hospital bed. It was the same bed that I had crawled into as a child when I needed to be close to him or to my mother, the bed where we snuggled and watched TV and shared many casual and intimate moments of family life. The house was completely silent, and the sound of Dad's breathing dominated the atmosphere in the room. It didn't appear to be requiring a lot of effort; his body was just alternately inhaling and exhaling, not quite ready to give up. In the dim light he looked very peaceful and handsome, and I had the strong sense that he was not struggling in any way.

> *Rejoice, for his time of salvation is near. The body is a weight on the soul and when it is shed he will soar to great heights. Your father will be greeted by his own loving guides, and know that great care will be taken to welcome his spirit with loving embraces. Bathe him in your love from head to toe. Carry him upward and beyond on the wave of emotion. Let love and gratitude guide him out of this world.*

At nine o'clock I drifted off to sleep. I don't know what woke me up again, but I looked at the clock and discovered that it was ten minutes after midnight. I was surprised that so much time had passed, and I quickly turned to see if Dad had slipped away when I wasn't looking. He was still alive but there had definitely been a change. His breathing had become very shallow and slow. Something in me knew the end was near. I gave him a dose of morphine to help him breathe more easily, as I had been instructed, and I knew the moment had come.

Say your most heartfelt prayer; one befitting this loving father and healer of your soul. He is trapped between two worlds and you can set him free by guiding him to the doorway. Visualize this now. He is disappearing into the other world very gradually. He is reluctant to go and leave you behind. Pray for the deliverance of his soul into God's hands. Place yourself in awe of the experience of dying—do not dread it. Rejoice, for his spirit is about to be set free; it is fitting he should be liberated and allowed to rest.

I felt very calm as I took my place in a chair at his side, and put on headphones. While I listened to the *Fauré Requiem* the funeral mass lifted my soul, and for the last time I reached over and grasped my father's hand.

The experience of death makes itself known. It has transformative powers like no other experience in human life. It creates a shift in awareness that causes those who are left behind, to die to their previous understanding. Any discomfort felt is due to resistance and fear. Stand in awe. Allow it to change you. Deeply respect its powers and give thanks for the healing that occurs.

I talked to him, I prayed, and at six minutes past one in the morning on July 9, I held his hand and watched him peacefully take his last breath.

Come with Me to where there is no pain and no earthly care. Your future is in My hands. Be carried by My love. Surrender to Me and know peace.

One minute he was breathing, and the next minute he was not. There was no thunderbolt, no fearful emotion present. I prayed, "Take heart, dear one. Your time is here. God bless you."

Behold the working of the Lord. Your father's time on earth has passed. Know that he returns to the Source of all Life. On the other side of death is new life. Rejoice, for you have found the key to your earthly existence; it is a step along the way in a continuum of life. Show reverence for what you have just witnessed. You have been given a glimpse of eternity and for that opportunity you should give thanks to God.

A Sign

When I got up to tell my mother it was over, I paused at the foot of the bed to take a last, lingering look. This time I knew it was all right to leave the room, and I didn't feel I was abandoning him. He had passed through the crack between the worlds; he had found the door and was on the other side.

We called hospice and asked them to send a nurse to declare him officially dead, and it was two-thirty in the morning before she finally left. When the mortuary picked up Dad's body, I didn't watch as it was zipped into a black bag and wheeled out on a gurney. I just caught a glimpse of it passing the open door of the room in which I was sitting with my mother. I wanted to keep the memory of his peaceful repose as my last image of him.

We tried to get some rest then, and I slept for a few hours on the couch in the living room. I did not want to spend any more time in the bedroom and risk reliving the last few days. I had had enough of death and dying, and when I awoke at dawn, I was seized by a very strong impulse to breathe fresh air and to see a tree or a flower . . . something alive and growing.

For five days I had literally stared into the face of death, and now I hungered for signs of life. I got up, quietly left the house, and went for a walk. I hadn't gone more than three blocks when, to my complete surprise, I received what I recognized as an unmistakable sign from my father.

I was strolling through Leisure World, the retirement village where my parents had lived for fourteen years. When they moved there from Chicago, they joined the 20,000 residents who had come from every part of the country, leaving behind children, grandchildren, friends and careers, in search of the perfect place to live out the rest of their days. Southern California's climate was ideal, as were the many appealing features of this well-designed environment. They were attracted by the security of the gated community; the perfectly maintained and landscaped grounds bursting with the beauty of perpetually blooming tropical flowers and trees; excellent health care facilities that included a convenient hospital with an abundance of doctors and pharmacies; hourly shuttle buses to local shopping centers; and a large variety of recreational opportunities.

There are swimming pools, tennis courts, ceramics studios, golf courses, clubhouses, bridge clubs, mah jong games, dance lessons, bird-watching clubs, concerts and much more. Outwardly, Leisure World looks like paradise. You don't begin noticing that something is not quite right until you've spent a few days there, and the feeling that something is missing starts creeping over you. After a while you ache to see someone who is in a different stage of life, because everyone there is fifty-five or older.

There is no one who is middle aged; there are no teenagers, no children. This situation sent my parents and their friends on frequent trips to the nearby mall, to soak up the sight of babies toddling along on shaky legs, or to coo at infants passing by in strollers. Parking themselves on benches, they spoke to the passing parade of young mothers, and pinched their babies' cheeks. My mother engaged in her favorite pastime of striking up conversations with pregnant women and (to their delight) predicting the sex of their unborn children by detecting the presence or absence of creases in their chins.

It was a mild, cloudy morning shortly after sunrise, and a slight fog was hanging in the air. I floated down the sidewalk in a daze, seeing familiar objects for the first time. The world of the living was like a dream to me after so many days of being shut in with death. At this early hour very few people were out on the street, but suddenly I found myself walking toward a rare sight. A woman pushing a stroller with two babies was heading toward me . . . right there in Leisure World! My heart danced with joy at the sight of them.

After so many hours of staring at my elderly, dying father, it was a huge relief to look into the face of human beings at the beginning of life. The twins smiled, and then suddenly the awareness hit and nearly knocked the wind out of me. Oh my God! I was looking at *twin girls*. This was more than a coincidence! First I found myself on the same airplane with the conjoined twins who had haunted me for months, and who were for me the symbol of two human beings bound together in suffering.

Now, within hours of my father's death, I was having this unlikely encounter with happy, carefree, perfectly formed twin girls. These girls, probably six months of age, were unfettered, free spirits. Something in me was touched very deeply by the sight of them, by the happiness and serenity I saw when they looked directly into my eyes.

No, this was not chance. In fourteen years of visiting my parents at Leisure World, I had never seen a child within the confines of its walls. Not until that moment. I was suddenly filled with an overwhelming feeling of joy and gratitude, because in the depths of my being, I knew my dad was letting me know he was at peace.

Eulogy

My father is a great and generous soul who spread goodness in his path and brought love to the lives of those he touched. I believe that greatness isn't measured by earthly occupations, but by the capacity for love and generosity of spirit. By this measure, my father is one of the great ones.

His gifts have been many, and were always given selflessly: he asked no reward as he walked through this life quietly sharing the generosity of his soul, and his existence taught many of us what our true capacity for love is.

He offered love to everyone he encountered . . . love, humor, and generosity, which extended into his last days. His final act of goodness and mercy was to spare his loved ones the pain of seeing him suffer. He is truly a great soul.

When I was here three weeks ago, I knew he had to live with the reality that he was dying, so I wanted to have some conversations with him that I hoped would offer him some comfort. I told him that he was one of the greatest teachers I've had in my life—and the most important one—because he taught me who I am. He taught me that love is at the core of my being . . . and he did that by loving me.

A few weeks ago I was talking to someone about the fact that my dad was dying. She asked me to tell her some of my childhood memories of him. I told her that one strong memory I had was what it was like to hold his hand. As a little girl he always felt like a giant to me, and when I reached up and put my hand in his, I always felt very safe. In one of our last conversations I told him that.

119

This morning I was lying awake and thinking about the significance of our holding hands . . . because I was holding his hand when he took his last breath. And it felt as if I were handing him up to God.

As much as our friends and family would like to keep him here, we can't. He will have to be with us in spirit only from now on. But a piece of us will always be together with him . . . because we're linked in love.

Pray for peace to come to your father's soul. Carry him off on waves of love. The funeral service will boost him on his way and give him the loving foundation he seeks, the platform he can take off from into his next place of rest.

Encase your feelings of sadness and grief in the awareness that liberation follows the physical existence. Freedom from pain and fear follows the soul as it continues on its journey back to God.

Part 2

*The Body Speaks,
the Mind Remembers,
and the
Heart Understands*

Chapter Five

Living in Two Worlds

It wasn't until my father had been dead for several years that I began to understand how all my life I have been going from room to room, following a distantly heard tune. I've opened many doors and peeked inside, trying to find the source of the sound. One winter night I became aware that I had always been searching outside myself, when all the time the sound was coming from within. Alone in the house, I awoke to a familiar tingling feeling that urged me to put pen to paper. As I wrote, I sensed that something I had been reaching for but was forever slipping away was now within my grasp.

The knowledge came into focus gradually, and as it did, a wave of contentment and joy swept over me. I had been running from death all my life, and when I stopped running and accepted its presence, confusion about the nature of my existence began to clear. I saw that the veil dropped over our eyes when we come into this life is very real and creates a distortion that is necessary to sustain our existence. I also realized how, because we have free will and are able to choose what we see, if we deliberately perpetuate the blurred vision, we find ourselves going against the current of life.

We are carried away from the source of our existence by the choices we make, and the more we fight, the more we're defeated. If we arrive at the point where we realize that death is inevitable and must be accepted, however, a calm resignation descends—like it did on me that frigid February night.

When we're born, we gain understanding of our physical environment as we learn to think our way into meaning. We begin to train our sights on the visible world and throw all the energy of our existence into making sense of it, because that is where our tools for survival lie in the first few years. What we see, hear, smell, taste, and touch must be categorized and classified and codified until our brains learn to function like computers, where all our sensory impressions are filed away in folders marked "memory and cognition." When we can understand and name the dangers of the world in which we live—electrical sockets, moving cars, high places—we can control our own destinies and choose to reach, with our will, for those actions that will perpetuate our survival.

We have encoded in our genes a desire to survive that is the physical body's highest priority. At the same time, it is also true that the spirit longs to be freed from its physical form. We are continually pulled from one desire to the other throughout our lives. We can't see where these paths are heading at first, and only gradually does the duality of our existence become apparent.

We hear the first whisperings at the time of adolescence, when we develop an awareness of ourselves as self-reliant beings, capable of making independent choices. At this time the physical aspect of our nature, which is pulled toward the earth and craves the gratification of its needs, begins to speak very loudly. It dominates our attention and our actions and continually pushes us farther, until cultivation of pleasure becomes a conscious life goal. In our affluent society, the basic needs of most citizens are met and we are no longer compelled to hunt for food and shelter. With life and liberty as givens, our existence becomes focused on the pursuit of happiness.

As we grow older, our indoctrination into the material world continues and is dominated by messages that equate money with the meaning of life. Money was once considered a means to an end; now its acquisition has become an end in itself with the highest value being placed not on effort, but on its reward. While an emphasis on tangible things is a necessary ingredient in our adaptation to life on this planet, it's not meant to continue indefinitely. Sadly, many of us don't move on, but instead remain preoccupied with creating comfort and the accumulation of material wealth.

Although we've realized an unprecedented level of prosperity, and our dreams of acquiring material possessions have largely come true, still we feel short-changed. Our lives seem empty and without meaning, because we've given money a measure of importance that is out of proportion to its proper place. With the material side of life receiving far too much attention, we've lost our balance and our perspective about the true nature of our existence: we live in two worlds—one which is visible and one which is not.

Fear of the Invisible

The affluence we enjoy has upheld our sense of the importance of the visible world, and we've come to put all our trust in whatever can be seen. The result is a weakening of our connection with the invisible, spiritual side of our nature.

All the questions within our souls carry with them their own answers. We are designed in such a way that our inner knowing will speak its truth and will compel us to listen. But to hear the wisdom of the soul when it speaks, we must become aware of that gentle voice whispering within and turn toward it to catch the sound. Its quiet messages are easily drowned out by the louder, flashier, and outwardly more attractive ones the entertainment media broadcast continually in our direction.

While these commercial messages do feed our hunger for survival, the promises of material wealth, power, and financial success only create a thirst for more of the same, which can never be quenched. As the noise of the broadcasts becomes louder and increasingly enticing, we find more and more ways to avoid taking seriously the voice that calls us to turn inward. We'd prefer not to tune in to a channel that plays reminders of our mortality. We're drawn to whatever station sustains our illusions about life, and skip over or mute the programs that contain allusions to death.

Many of us have had our sense of reality shaped by life as it is portrayed on television. Although there is no comparison between the true light emanating from each living being and the artificial glare emitted by the electronic screen, we stand in the light of the TV and worship the images we see there. But the false gods we worship are a reflection of our own desire to stay on the surface of life, and not of any deeper truth. It takes great strength and effort to transform ourselves into what we already are, rejecting the deceptions created by those who have had power over us and have transfixed our gaze on something that is not real. Along the way we have lost sight of the fact that it's pointless to become too attached to our shape, our activities or our possessions because they are all fleeting drops in an ocean of eternity.

At the core of our fears is an element of truth: the fact that our existence will end. We fear it because we only attach understanding and give meaning to what we can see. The intangible realms signify the terrifying experience of being swept away by a torrent of darkness into territory where we're out of control, where our identity is obliterated.

Aging in the Technology Age

When we're adults, we no longer seek refuge in the kinds of entertainment that transported us in childhood from the humdrum of our lives. We don't play the way we used to, imaginatively and with joy in the simplest act, because our imaginations have been ruthlessly devoured by the electronic images to which we make ourselves prey. Care is taken to see that we are continually being bombarded with noise, for the silence within has great power. We stage raids on our own houses, and steal from ourselves the ability to be silent, to feel joy from knowing how to be alone, and to sit still and wait for answers.

The pattern of our existence becomes interrupted by lies perpetuated in advertising, so we lose track easily of our direction and our perspective in life. Isolation caused by seclusion with electronic equipment and the habitual wearing of headphones disconnects us from one another, and from many of the traditions that mark time and show us our place in the community. Long hours of television viewing rob us of our ability to live complete emotional lives, because we're trading real life experiences for vicarious ones. We invest a tremendous amount of time in watching others live their fake lives, and spend a great deal of emotional currency on their fictional life circumstances.

But while we might weep when tragedy befalls a character in a soap opera, at the same time we throw up defenses around our own genuine emotions to protect ourselves. Instead of developing deep connections with loved ones in our real lives, we learn to construct pathways around our feelings and channel them away from us, directing them outward toward objects that are safe. We bury ourselves in televisions, Walkmans, DVD players, iPods, iPhones, CD players, MP3 players, BlackBerry devices, PCs, laptops, Blu-ray disc players or computer games.

The consequence of our intimacy with electronic devices is that our lives have become diminished and emotionally flattened; experiencing any intensity of feeling can cause us discomfort ranging from uneasiness and fear to disorientation and total emotional chaos. We're compelled to suspend strong feelings at all cost, for fear they will lead us into territory where we will not be in charge. Rather than traveling into the uncharted land of emotions and perhaps losing our way, we continually channel surf. That eliminates the need for engagement and the possibility of mining feelings we don't dare bring up to the surface.

When my father died of cancer, his brother was unable to come into the room and participate in Dad's last minutes on earth. At first I was angry and disappointed, until I realized he was not indifferent—he was just terrified.

He did not dare experience any of the natural responses because they made him susceptible to feelings from which he had protected himself all his life.

Several months later, when Uncle John watched Princess Diana's funeral on TV, I saw him cry his heart out. I was very puzzled at first, until I realized that it was safe for him to wrap his emotions around this media icon, because in doing that he was not crying for a real person, he was mourning an idea: a beautiful young princess being cut down in her prime. It was possible for him to grieve for someone to whom he was not actually related, because that was several layers removed from true sentiment, and as such, was not nearly as painful or threatening. It's a sad commentary on our TV-obsessed culture that we frequently only feel safe experiencing emotions when we are empathizing with people to whom we have no connection; namely, actors who are pretending to be feeling something in imaginary situations.

Our impulse for living is sucked away by the frequency of the sounds emitted by electronic machines, and our energy diminishes and starts to fall. Crashing at the bottom we begin to question the influence of these devices in our world, realizing that when we choose entertainment over life, we subvert the concept of free will and reduce our lives to channel surfing.

Embrace the Silence Within

There is a way that the perpetuation of superficiality by various institutions serves society; it keeps us from knowing who we really are. Search and destroy missions have been conducted where our hearts have been raided and robbed of their true feelings. Awaken to the knowledge that your house is being invaded! Don't be content to sleep through the invasion—arouse your being and take a stand against the attempt to keep your conscious mind riveted to the surface. Superficiality breeds rapidly and populates the world with empty shells: individuals whose true identities have been stolen. Don't allow yourself to become hypnotized by the medium of television, or its messages. Hang your hat on the hook marked "My Life." Take all there is of life, and don't settle for anything less!

Track your own true course, and resolve to miss the appropriate place no more. See your life as a bookcase, where everything you have put on display is there by your own design. When we dare to dust off the volumes on the shelves, underneath the layers of dirt obscuring our vision are many titles that contain our deepest secrets. Each item is unique, carefully chosen, and scrupulously placed.

If we turn away from the glare of the TV and shut off its constant noise, we become aware of a voice within telling us that our lives are bound by the limit put on them by physical death. Acknowledging this allows the meaning of our existence to surface. When we lay to rest the dependence on external reality that has become the life-sustaining drug of our culture, we stop building barriers around ourselves and the natural course our lives are meant to take. Only then, by using the guidance we receive from within and the faculty of free will, can we reach for the heights of which we are capable.

Inner Voice

There is a clock within each of us here on earth that is ticking our lives away. It makes a very subtle sound, which is not easy to hear, because we find ourselves surrounded by other, more distinctly audible noises. The ability to recognize this biological clock depends on our willingness to become aware of the limited amount of time we have between birth and physical death. The death of the body is real; it is an observable phenomenon. That the spirit continues to live is also a phenomenon that can be proven to be true, but different instruments are used to perform such a test.

The true sound of our spirit's voice can be heard throughout our lives, yet it can never be measured in decibels or tones. It's a sound that requires concentration to notice; it cannot be heard over the din of electronic clutter with which we surround ourselves. Yet those who are willing to listen find themselves guided toward activities that give a clear direction and purpose to their lives. They are in touch with a power great enough to steer them toward survival and away from death . . . or just the opposite.

We must begin to find a way to turn down the external noise and bring the perpetual motion of our physical beings to a stop. Hold still! Be quiet! If we do this long enough we allow the power of the spirit to break through the interference that has been built around it. Putting that voice at the center of our lives means turning up the volume within and ignoring the idle temptations to be distracted, lose focus, tune out, ignore, and fear the sound that can drive us into the ground of our being—to wait until the power within becomes stronger than what surrounds us.

The meaning of all life lies between the lines and cannot be perceived or interpreted by reason alone, nor by any of the physical senses, for their job is to teach us by classifying everything we experience into categories of meaning. But true wisdom defies labeling. Genuine understanding of the relationships between living things and their environment and the Source of all meaning— these are readily accessible to the human being, but only through a faculty we have been taught to ignore. Inner Teacher, Authentic Self, Higher Self, Source, Spirit, Divine Wisdom, Inner Voice: whatever label we attach to it, it is a force that can move our lives toward completion in the truest sense of the word. Not the end, but the finishing touch, the results we came here to achieve.

When we understand that our lives are directed from

within and bring us into those precise circumstances that will shed clarity and light where there is none, we comprehend the duration and purpose of our time here. It is a limited period in which we can unearth the missing links in our quest for wholeness. Seen from this perspective, every trial, every illness, every misfortune is not a punishment, but a teacher and an opportunity to lift ourselves higher than the circumstances of our lives and propel ourselves into a state of pure knowing and bliss.

When we no longer feel the separation of our identity into segregated parts—the professional, the parent, the spouse, the gardener, the community leader, the grandparent—the life we have created will serve one purpose: to enable us to become an integrated person who lives by following an inner compass. When we are grounded like this, in the deepest part of our being, then the way to live harmoniously and happily becomes clear. No amount of looking away from the reality of the paradoxes inherent in our life on earth can help us understand how to live.

Chapter Six

Living with Integrity

*D*o not pretend that you cannot see death's presence as a force in your own life, or the integrity of your existence will be compromised. Capture in every detail of living the full capacity for the enjoyment of truth.

The sounding board of integrity lies deep within the soul of each individual and carries chords that harmonize the different strains of our lives. We make our level of understanding and wisdom known to ourselves by the tasks we choose to perform; beliefs present themselves in our actions and our actions reflect our beliefs. When the actions we choose strike a resonant chord, we are emboldened to continue along the path we are on. But if there is an absence of sonority, the poverty of sound and resonance hurts the inner ear and causes us to turn away, seeking the harmony of the true sound's note.

The discord that results when we choose the wrong path can be heard and felt by all of the antennae with which we are equipped. We are looking for the chamber in which to sound the right notes; where the echo that returns steers us onto the right course; where the quality of our experience creates an alignment of body, mind, and spirit and brings the message from our soul that we are on the right track. When the interference in our head becomes still, the harmony of our being can be heard and given the chance to sweep us away with the beauty of its song.

Sometimes we recognize the lack of attunement when we are striking the wrong chord, but we just don't know what we are hearing. To step into the fullness of life we must switch to another frequency and pattern our lives after a different sound. It will become clear as a bell in time, and its sweet note will signal that all is well. All it takes is a shift in orientation from the resonance of material well-being to a resonance offering hope for the future and nurturance for the soul. When we switch course and make these things our goals, we cannot chase a false identity and all the unhappiness and grief that can bring.

Living with the fullness of life expands every minute into a lifetime, and transports us into the here and now. The happiness and gratification we are searching for are before us in many different guises—the next sink we clean, the meal we eat, the broken appliance we repair. Stepping into the present moment allows us to fulfill our destiny from one second to the next, without postponement.

No matter how loud we turn up the volume, nothing will drown out the sound of death knocking at the door. It can only be embraced; embraced with the same readiness with which we attempt to face every other aspect of our lives. And the equipment we need to accomplish this task is polished and prepared throughout a lifetime of living with integrity—turning toward the sound that resonates most deeply within the chambers of the soul.

Connections on the Web of Life

Witness the connections between all living things above all else. Genuine delight at the simple things in life will bring you in contact with what is meaningful and true for you. When the connections reveal themselves between the lines, the fabric of life begins to make itself known. Remember to focus your attention on the connections between the lines, not on the main attractions, and move outward from there. Right action stems from adherence to the highest path and not from the desire to gain power and control. Hold fast to these beliefs and power yourself forward on wings of love.

The web of life is a reality. There are knots woven into the fabric, which snag each of us at different times in our lives. Difficulties we experience along the road of life represent the need to learn to unravel the knots. When we succeed in accomplishing this, we glide by the obstacles easily and no longer have to fabricate delicate situations in which we can become trapped. Often we, ourselves, create the opportunities for learning that we require.

We make connections with others at the moment we are conceived. Our ability to thrive depends on a healthy physical and psychic interrelationship with another's being; that of the mother, whose body and soul nourish us. We graduate to a more direct link with the broad physical environment when we're born and are forced to depend on the quality of air, purity of water, and nourishment of the food available.

Our social patterns also reflect a healthy dependency on the bonds we make. To remain in touch with our own feelings, we must stay linked to the emanations of others. We wear in our emotional costumes the garments with which others clothe us early in life. Our mothers and fathers not only dress our bodies, they also cloak our naked souls in emotional vestments; we wear their love and affection, their pride, their generosity of spirit. The threads of these emotions weave raiments that shield and protect us, and reveal an identity with which we learn to feel comfortable and by which we become known. We stand solidly behind the portrayal of ourselves that we glimpse every time we interact with others and see our reflections returned to us. This delicate interplay of emotions continues throughout our lives as long as we maintain healthy connections to one another.

We weave in and out of our relationships the blueprint of patterns that were drawn before we were born. We need to know ourselves, and we come to understand who we are only when we cross-weave our own strands with the cords of life being woven by others. In the same way that we become intricately bound with the people and environment with which we interact, we always remain tied to the deeper weave at the foundation of our existence.

Although we tear ourselves apart trying to slow down or obliterate awarenesses from within that evoke the deeper meaning of our lives, we can carry the charade only so far, until we drop the load. In contrast, we grow in understanding every time we acknowledge the alliance that exists between ourselves and different life forms. To know and accept that the origin of our existence is also a seed, not unlike plant forms, floating on the river of life until it washes ashore exactly where it is meant to land—to become fertile, germinate, and eventually bear fruit—means we place ourselves on the web of life where we are meant to be. We cannot keep ourselves bottled inside the illusion that ours is the one manifestation of life that defies death, decay, and destruction. Nature dictates certain laws that cannot be changed even when we choose to ignore them.

Seeing and Looking Away:
the Conjoined Twins

When we are willing to look at rather than avert our glances from those things of which we are afraid, the enormous power they have over us is transformed. The conjoined twins' startling deformity set in motion a wave of energy that brought me closer to what was most strongly repelling me. The desire to both look at them and look away was present at once within me. The energy pattern of that response became a pendulum I was riding, as I was continually drawn toward the awareness of death and compelled to look away. They were visible reminders for me of the duality of our existence, and I've often thought of what a remarkable coincidence it was to see them on the plane that day.

Those girls came to symbolize for me the undeniable paradox that informs our lives: even as we are born we are beginning to die. They provide poignant reminders of the co-existence of life and death, light and dark, good and evil, clarity and illusion. We inhabit a body and are pulled toward the earth and the task of caring for its physical needs, while also being drawn toward the world of the spirit and our need to know the source of our existence and our relation to the Creator. This is the conflict of the sacred and the profane into which we are born.

As inhabitants of the world, our lives are constrained by physical laws and restraints, one of which is a need to understand all aspects of our existence and a simultaneous fear and dread of the same. The deepest stirrings of the soul bring with them a sense of alarm, and while we are attracted to these inner truths, we are also repelled by them. In each one of us lies the capacity to embrace the truths of our existence and the desire to escape them. Only when we learn to position ourselves where our interests lie will we be open and willing to face them.

The duality of our existence is represented by our emotions. As we go back and forth on the "pro and con" level, we are pulled between despair and hope, sadness and joy, hatred and love. The pull is in the direction of the mystery, toward the unanswered questions: the attempt to know where we came from and where we will go when life is over. The direction and the need to know are undeniable. When we come to rest in the middle we have found the proper posture—a balance between earthly concerns and spiritual matters.

Seeing the conjoined twins, I was compelled to refrain from wrapping myself in my customary illusions because they pounded the truth into me every moment I spent gazing at their unusual physical form. They demanded to be heard and seen; it was virtually impossible to look past them and pretend they didn't exist. The power their presence had over me was formidable. The intensity of the sight of those two human beings tragically bound together had the effect of eradicating blind spots I had carefully cultivated over the years. Nothing short of this radical accident of nature could have gripped me so strongly and affected me so deeply as to heal the wounds I had created by "looking away" from what I refused to see.

Being sealed in the cabin of that DC 9 with them was a gift of major proportions that only became recognizable many months after the event. My body and soul were given a jolt that closed the gaps in the emotional framework of my inner life. Thanks to them I began to heal, and I recognize what a truly special presence they are and a gift to this life which they are walking through, awkwardly joined together as they are.

Who cannot recognize the strength it takes to face the shocked stares of those who are unable to look away? We need what they have; the ability to travel with courage through life's darkest valleys and to know that we can face any situation thrown in our path. We want this and at the same time are repelled by the thought of having to live this way. All the secrets hidden in our souls are drawn forth and revealed by being exposed to these extraordinary creatures.

My gratitude goes out to these girls who brought me in contact with parts of myself that I didn't know existed. After seeing them, I wasn't able to hide from my fears, and I found a connection to my own dark side. To actually stand on the threshold of my fears and embrace that darkness created a quality of wholeness that had been missing. These unique beings have a strange power— they can bring transformation and beauty into the world through the deformity that they are destined to bear. I feel linked to them by a chain of events that have touched me at the deepest level.

I have begun to realize what instruments of healing they were, how they helped me find a missing piece of my existence and put it in place. I no longer see them as deformed, but as perfectly complete: yin and yang. I thank them for teaching me about wholeness. I am connected to their lives in ways I do not understand. We are joined together forever.

Things Change; Life Never Ends

The seasons change and we hardly look up and notice. Radical shifts in the slant of the light occur, temperatures drop, leaves fall, and bees hungrily milk the blossoms of their last drops of nectar, driven by the awareness of the approaching first frost.

No matter how we try to deny it, for all creatures time moves forward and we find inside of us signals that mark its passage. New awarenesses appear within the heart and mind of each individual, floating into consciousness and calibrating our wisdom with instruments that measure the passage of time: the drooping of skin, the greying of hair, the rapid release of memories from the brain trapping us in the present.

Soon you will belong only to the moment—the moment

when your ship leaves this shore. Acknowledge the passage of time and let life's energy carry you to your destiny. The journey is everything! Wash along with the waves and be tossed about in the waters of life. Let yourself be taken into every cavity of existence . . . the highs and lows and the welcome and unwelcome experiences and emotions. The shifts back and forth that thrust you against the rough contours of life batter you until you easily reshape into the form you are now meant to take.

Cradle yourself in the arms of the Earth Mother and allow her to transport you away to your new abode, far from the discomfort and insecurity of childhood and onto the back porch, where you were always at home.

While sitting at my father's side in the last days of his life, I rarely took my eyes off him. I was looking for any sign that he needed my help, and I was afraid if I looked away I would miss it. With my attention riveted on him, I witnessed the transformation of his body as he died, and in the process one of life's most basic truths was revealed to me . . . things change.

Babies grow, leaves fall from the trees, the earth revolves around the sun and day changes into night—we're born and then we die. Always hold up a mirror to nature to see the finest detail. Your own reflection is a source of wisdom and understanding. Catch the meaning behind the variety of life and the changes in appearance we all go through. The changes are endless and can be observed from the moment of birth; like it or not, your metabolism is speeding toward its conclusion.

Denying the changes are taking place and not accepting with grace the reality of aging is what produces the fear that will come back to haunt us at the time of our deaths. If we put the brakes on in a rapidly moving vehicle it spins out of control; we create the same effect when we throw up a roadblock of resistance and deny the inevitable end of life. When we resist, we slam into a concrete wall because the truth cannot be shattered.

Death is waiting for us at the other end of life and if we don't want to spin out of control, we must steer ourselves very deliberately toward it; we must reach for it and appreciate its existence. Recognize that because it prevails between the lines, death elevates to high visibility aspects of life that we love to acknowledge—freedom, wonder, beauty, joy, the miracle of birth and the innocence of a child. These only catch our attention because we are willing to be touched by them and notice their qualities. But death provides the contrast that illuminates the vibrant qualities of life, and if we pretend that its not waiting for us, we cannot appreciate the wonders of our existence.

Putting all value on what seems, rather than what is between the lines that supports and shines a light on the obvious, results in misunderstanding. I felt my awareness of the transitory nature of our earthly existence deepen as I watched the changes my father went through. The great lesson that was seeping into my consciousness is that if things change constantly, there is no end to the changes.

As my father left his body behind, a part of me went with him; I realized my connection to the other side of life and felt the continuum very clearly. Staring at his form, as he dissolved into another state of being, strengthened the outline and gave clarity to my own boundaries. Looking into the face of death eliminated the fear that had cast

Part 3

Finding the Path
We're Already On

Chapter Seven

Death is a Teacher and a Friend

I'm convinced that each one of us, when we are born, is set on a path that we are meant to follow. Our lives take us in search of it, and as we get older its location becomes increasingly clear. We develop an inner sense that corrects our direction if we go astray, and when we make a slight diversion off our true course, an alarm goes off. It makes a nearly imperceptible sound at first, but the more we pay attention, the easier it is to notice.

It may manifest as doubt and discomfort, questioning why we are doing what we are doing, and why we are in that particular situation to begin with. It may feel as if we are wearing somebody else's skin rather than our own. It creates enough of a discomfort of the spirit that we either have to dodge the sensations coming our way or correct our course and get back on track. We become derailed when we don't make choices that allow us to feel whole, pursuing our true purpose. Then, living requires a tremendous energy output, as we put all our effort into carrying out the design of a life that is not really a good fit for us.

I have learned that death is a teacher and a friend because it has the power to illuminate the proper course of action, when it intrudes on our fantasies and forces us to abandon our illusions. In its presence, a starkly lit path is laid before us and our choices become brilliantly clear. There has never been a time in my life when I felt so guided by courage and strength as when I encountered death, and all I had to do was surrender to the inevitable power of change that carries us through life. Never were the rules so clear, the boundaries and definition of my path so transparent. I knew exactly each step I was meant to take because I was willing to look at where I was heading: toward the final destination, which is death. To my surprise, I discovered that at the same time I was letting go of my father's life, I found the depth of my own life increasing.

We have to be willing to see the truth—that death will come to all of us. What we believe comes after death will likely influence our attitude toward accepting it. Some of us believe it is the end of existence, and so the prospect of death is especially terrifying. Some of us feel, triggered in the deepest layers of emotion, a connection to sensations that reveal truths so stirring in their integrity that they are beyond our intellect's capacity to grasp their meaning. It's as if there are vibrations floating between time and space (to which we can connect with our inner receptors) that have none of the limitations of our sense organs, because the medium through which they are received is something other than the brain.

The tuning fork that sends out the vibrations is the Universal Soul of Consciousness. It is our destiny to receive these pulsations of sound, and to benefit from their wisdom we must choose to translate them into actions that will steer our course in the direction of our intended path.

Leaving the path of materialism seems contrary to the lessons of survival that we are taught by society. But the social self must serve one master and the spiritual self another. True integration of the two aspects of the self is the goal for which we must strive. Connecting the aspirations of the social self with the guiding principles of the inner life reconciles seeming disparities and leads to a core of integrity that guides us to revelations of the truths that govern our existence. When we pursue integrity, we come face to face with the fact of death.

We need to walk a path of integrity and not duck when something unfriendly or uncomfortable comes our way. We must face problems head on with our own personal truth and not expect to find solutions anywhere but within ourselves; we have often created the problem in order to supply the opportunity needed for making the necessary correction. We challenge ourselves repeatedly by creating circumstances that seem to be beyond our control, but are actually just the opposite. When we learn to meet each situation with the right combination of power and surrender, the balance in our own beings will draw energies of equanimity into the situation.

Make no mistake—everything is well within our control. When we are in a difficult situation, the layers within our deepest self are shifting and we experience a sense of disorientation and of loss. We cannot know how we'll react beforehand, but when challenged by adversity, our spirits may become recharged, making us feel alive with possibilities. We can learn to recognize these situations as opportunities knocking on the door and gathering our potential. These concentrated energies are at our disposal and can be reached at any given time by exercising our free will. Saving our energy for exactly the right choice builds new patterns and allows us to recreate ourselves each and every minute. The actions we have chosen will mark a new way of being, and knowing how to make the right choice will open the door we are meant to walk through.

When our goal becomes acknowledging that we will reach the end of our lives, then each step we take turns into a deliberate positioning on our true course and allows us to be carried along the stream of life. However, if we seek out divergent paths that require us to clear the brush and create a new direction, the energy required to tame the wilderness expends the creative energies in our souls. Surrendering to the path of least resistance collects strength and allows us to gather ourselves into the fullness of our nature and express with exactness and richness the depth of our beings. Although it seems like a great paradox, the path that directs us toward an awareness of death and apparent destruction fulfills the manifestation of our spirits with the complete expression of our true selves and all its creative potential.

Each event in our lives can draw us into preparation for expansion into the hereafter if we become certain of the direction in which we are going. By consciously heading toward our death, we have a purpose before us that keeps us set on course. We take each step with certainty and feel the integrity of the truth guiding our feet. We all seek not to stumble and fall; death can teach us how to walk with strength, conviction and sure-footedness.

Mysteries 101:
Acknowledging the Teacher Within

Wisdom in our culture is very plentiful. We are taken on journeys with every possible type of guide, and for the price of a workshop or a series of classes we can buy whatever it is we want to know.

It also a fact that truth and wisdom are freely

available to anyone who wants to enroll in the class of life. There are no mysteries that can't be understood, no visions that cannot be seen, and no truths that cannot be comprehended by the wisdom of the soul. We need only acknowledge the guidance of the teacher within in order to enroll ourselves in the course.

Step aside . . . and before you know it, the train will leave from the station and you'll be on it. You'll be carried to every port of call you can imagine to see sights and experience adventures you never thought possible.

Bland is cheap, but rich and deep cannot be purchased. You are one with every vision, with every sound, with every spice, with every scent, with every whole experience, and with all the collective knowledge and wisdom accumulated over eons. We must have the courage to embrace our identities and claim our birthright. We have only to be willing to open the door and walk through, trusting that we'll be guided where we're meant to go.

The heart is longing to reveal its wisdom. The knowledge of how to live and how to die is locked in its chambers. The wisdom of the soul holds the key to unlocking those doors . . . and we're on a treasure hunt to find it. The clues are being given daily, and when we're ready to be receptive, they can be heard. If we take the time to listen and make the time in our lives for quiet and contemplation, our hearts will speak their truth.

We carry encoded in our beings a longing to reveal the secrets of life and the mysteries of death. The answers are in plain sight for all to see. The breeze whispers them, the birds tell us in their song, the earth underneath our feet provides the foundation for our understanding. There is no secret code that is not already in our hands. All life supports mutual understanding, and knowing is awakened when we position ourselves in the community of life, as learners and seekers.

Enjoy the Journey

Claim the knowing that is already within. Preparation for death continues throughout our lifetime and culminates with the physical expulsion of the body's useless garment. Trade in the old for the new—this is the theme that is repeated constantly throughout life. Every cell in the body is being continually renewed; physical death of the old and transformation into the new is a fact of life. The garment we cast off at the end of life is not the same that we have carried since we were born.

At the moment of birth, a pattern was born that continues without interruption throughout the course of our lives. Waves of energy course through our field and transport us ever forward into the stream of our energetic existence. Life does not depend on our understanding it, but when we can grasp what is happening, we can ride the train and be carried along.

Trying to prove to ourselves that the train of life is carrying us in the opposite direction from its true destination brings us crashing down into the path of the next train—a moving vehicle that stops for no one. If we refuse to allow ourselves to be carried, we will be dragged along, because there's no getting off. We will be transported no matter what, and whether we choose to go along for the ride, or choose to resist, the train never stops.

The impulse of Creation moves always in the direction of new life and does not come grinding to a halt simply because we refuse to accept the movement, which is clearly visible and there for us to see. The joy in life comes from experiencing the ride, rather than resisting the pull. Like feeling the bumps in the road that lift your stomach and create a pleasant sensation, ride the waves of each new challenge and put forth all the strength you have . . . not to resist death, but to hang on for dear life so you can delight in the ride. We will become what we are meant to be, and whether we enjoy the journey depends on our ability to surrender to the movement that is carrying us forward.

Death's Gift

We take much for granted in life, because we assume there will always be another day to pay attention to the beauty around us, or to alter or elevate the quality of our relationships with those we love. The illusion that life on earth never ends allows us to pretend we can continue as we are forever. The gift that death has to offer is the awareness that all pleasure is finite, all beauty is transient, as well as the knowledge that we will not be here forever to work through our problems with others.

So acknowledge the presence of those you love, and let go of life in the sweetest way you know how. Live your life so you have no regrets. Honor your spouse or partner, your children, your friends. Never resort to violent acts or bring ruthless thoughts into the realm of your being. Draw down the love in every situation and replace vengeance with peaceful, loving vibrations. Admit to yourself that life is fleeting and all things as we know them will come to an end. Out of the awareness of the endings, create new beginnings. Begin to fill out your own form by making choices that allow you to control your own existence. Respect your loved ones and elevate your actions to reflect the highest principles of living: show love, respect, and honor for all life. Waste no energy on vanity or pride; be generous and giving and pursue the highest purpose in all you do.

Living Well/Dying Well

Living well involves learning to give up control. Surrender is the key word for your life. Bring all you know into the room and allow it to surround you. Furnish your house with all your blessings and bask in their glow. Don't cut short the benefits of the moment by preparing for what will come next. Be ever prepared to move into the new, but stay firmly anchored in the present. When you can balance keeping your attention on present details with being ready for whatever will come next, you will have achieved the proper balance for living well.

Dying well involves the same technique: not being afraid to receive the rays of information that are being sent to you and resisting the impulse to escape the pull into the next layer.

You are always bridging the known and the unknown and must release control in order to find freedom. The lessons on how to die well abound in every phase of life.

Stay grounded in the present but surrender to the pull of where you are being taken by the call of your inner voice. Find within you the still place where that call resides, and move forward in its direction with intention.

You are continually being shown the way that will lead you to the unfolding of a life plan designed for your highest good. Reach for the goals that are true for you, and not those imposed on you by others. The sound of your inner voice is drowned out by noises in the world. Follow the resonance of the frequency that pulls you toward the sound.

Contemplate the end of life without fear. It is time for you to take your place in this greater truth: life doesn't end, it only continues in a never-ending spiral of evolution.

Those who do not comprehend the fact of change are rooted in unreality. Pass on to a higher understanding of the order of life and feel the awareness of the transitory nature of this earthly existence in every act you undertake.

Fill the time you have left with all the good works that you can manage to perform. Prepare yourself for your passage by learning increasingly to trust; know that the time and the date of your death have been predetermined. The narrow escapes and missed accidents are no accident. They are evidence of the path that takes you around death and moves you forward toward the circumstances of your own unique destiny.

Facing death opens a sensor that is finely tuned to the pulse of the living. The gentle wave of creation pulses relentlessly and moves waves of energy through all life forms. Release the fearful responses that have been conditioned by previous experiences. Play no longer the game of defensiveness. Bleed when you hurt yourself and cry when you are in pain.

Believe that this is where death's door is leading— to the source of your existence and salvation from the trials and tribulations of life on the earth. Make no mistake that the image from your perspective is inverted. From where you stand, in your earthly costume, it appears that life is coming to an end. Know that the secret cannot be seen. In the dissolution of the body, the spirit is freed and liberation and joy are the end result of passing through death's door. This cannot be known early in life because you must remain focused on the goal of survival rather than passing out of this existence. When you have carried the burden of living long enough, the prospect of laying it down turns your sight inward, and a fork in the road appears.

Surrender to all emotions and remember that love guides the way and lights your path into the future. Your inner life has been brought into the gentle wave of creation. There's a quiet knowing that whispers its truth to you. You can only hear it in the silence of your heart. Be quiet. Be still. Be open and aware. Love is all around you. Embody it. Let it bake itself onto your awareness. Share it and give it forth.

Soul Power is the Sole Power

Walk through life with your head held high. Look death in the eye—you must continue to do so and your fears will fade. After death, fear will be vanquished. It is only a condition of earthly existence. You are not trapped; you will be released eventually into the loving arms of the Creator. Wrap your trust and love around your belief in God as you have never done before. Know that death comes from the Creator, as well as life, so you must accept it lovingly.

The true test of courage comes in the face of death. All the rest has been a game. Strengthen! Draw down the love, hand up your fear, and become what you are meant to be. Belong to the company of mature adults who know the joy of living and the inevitability of their dying—and who move into the unknown in a state of joy.

Give away no more the responsibility of living your own life and accepting your death. As you travel the journey of life, don't just go through the motions . . . BE the journey.

Climb aboard the train of life and grab onto your hat!

The Author

Georgia Weithe, M.Ed., is a teacher, educational consultant, alternative healer and artist. She has taught in settings ranging from public and private schools to colleges and universities, and consulted with educational institutions, social service and non-profit organizations. For ten years she has been a facilitator in the Center for Courage and Renewal's *Courage To Teach* program, created under the auspices of the Fetzer Institute. The main thrust of her work, in all domains, has been guiding people back to themselves. In a culture where most people are afraid of dying, the logical next step for this pilgrim spirit is to guide us into the unexplored territory of death, so we can face what lies ahead without fear.

Her credentials for writing about death come from a lifelong curiosity about the topic, and from her intimate contact with her father as he traveled his end-of-life journey. Sitting at his side while he lay dying, the experience of staring into the face of death taught her that death is a teacher we can all learn to befriend, and that only when we do, will we truly be able to enjoy the experience of living.